Quantum Sorcery

The Science of Chaos Magic

Quantum Sorcery

The Science of Chaos Magic

Dave Smith

Megalithica Books

Stafford, UK

Quantum Sorcery: The Science of Chaos Magic by Dave
Smith © 2021 Third edition

ISBN 978-1-912241-19-4

Catalogue Number: MB0211

Cover Art and Design: Danielle Lainton
Editor: Storm Constantine and Danielle Lainton
Layout: Storm Constantine and Danielle Lainton

Set in Book Antiqua and High Tower Text

A Megalithica Books Publication
An imprint of Immanion Press

www.immanion-press.com
info@immanion-press.com

Contents

Foreword

There are many approaches to magic. Over the decades that I have personally studied various systems, I have come across everything from completely faith-based magic to empiric scientific approaches, yet I was constantly beset with one question throughout my younger life that wouldn't begin to be resolved until the late 1980s; what makes the magic work? When I came across the disciplines within chaos magic theory, things began to fall into place. Here was a practical approach to magic that went beyond the limitations of ordinary science, yet refused to get lost in the airy fairy new age belief systems even though the magic might well draw from either extreme to formulate a result. Harnessing the ultimate power of the human mind as the basis of magic made sense with even an elementary concept of quantum physics.

Somewhere along my journey I began to correspond with Dave Smith. I believe this began in the Chaosmagic.Com community where I used to spend much more time before life as a film producer tore me away from too many idle hours of internet surfing. That too was an act of chaos. But although my correspondence may be less frequent, keeping some contact with those with whom I have discussed concepts of magic reminds me that there are others who share my question. Dave writes in the introduction to *Quantum Sorcery* in very similar words to my own from all those years ago, "what is the underlying mechanism by which the Will causes physical change in the universe?"

Oddly, despite my interest in chaos magic, I have never set foot in a physics class. The concepts make perfect sense to me when applied to magic, but I rely on people like Dave to investigate the links to traditional science. My studies may have taken me through chaos science and probability as well as alchemy, but a transient life has left a few gaps in my formal education which I am only motivated to fill when I find real life application for the information. Hence, my understanding of physics is largely coloured by its application to magic. It is always an honour to be asked to write a foreword for a book that you would like to have written yourself. Reading through the first section of this one is like reading the book I would wish to write if I had the time to do the research and to remember all of the materials I have studied over the years. The history of magic and the importance of the references to *The Emerald Tablet* in particular is something that many young magicians seem to miss out on in these days of instant gratification and television advert conditioned attention spans.

A good grounding in historic information is still valuable for the magician, even with the quick success ratio of Austin Osman Spare's popularised sigil methods. One doesn't have to follow the methods of historic magic or dead magicians to benefit from their example. Then of course there are the magicians still among us, the early chaos magicians like Peter J Carroll who began exploring the concepts of Austin Osman Spare and applying recent scientific theory to the practise of magic. Such magicians have forged new paths in modern magic, making it easier for the new magician to access workable information and to apply it to a world that is very unlike that of the historic Alchemists and Kabbalists. With more understanding of science, there is more understanding of magic.

It is when we get to the more scientific concepts behind magic in the second part of this book that I see the book that I couldn't have written. Yet, the clear and concise way in which Dave Smith has explained the history and concepts of physics leaves me feeling that I've definitely learned something of importance, and that is the goal of any non-fiction book. With the higher awareness that internet chaos magic has spread, I think it is time for this book. Books that do little more than re-hash the writings of Peter Carroll, Timothy Leary, and Robert Anton Wilson have appeared periodically since the late 1970's. I've avoided such an approach myself.

Quantum Sorcery is the first book I've seen for some time that delves right into the science behind the magic, and provides answers to the questions I was asking so long ago. I will make no attempt to paraphrase here, but leave the reader to savour the words of the author himself. The concepts of physics are inextricable from practical magic. Recognising that fact has become the arena of the chaos magician. Far from being dead, chaos magic has evolved to encompass the rapidly increasing information of the modern age and the changes in society that inevitably affect the growth of magical concept and community.

Parts of this book are like embracing an old friend. As I read about Lorenz and Mandelbrot, I am reminded of the ideas that stimulated my curiosity more than a decade ago when I first delved into the classic books like James Gleick's *Chaos: The Making of a New Science* and found that I was able to apply the concepts to magic. Some of the directions that internet chaos magic has travelled have interested me less perhaps, but always there has been fresh perspective and a plethora of ideas to be found to build on the basic concepts that make the magic work.

The approach of every magician is different. We draw on our own interests and experience. But it is in understanding the basic mechanics of magic and science that we are able to apply that experience to methods that will work for us individually. The work you are about to read may well be the only book you will ever need to accomplish this. After that, it's just a matter of practical application.

Jaq D Hawkins
April, 2006

Preface to the Third Edition

I have learned a great deal since I began the work that eventually became the first edition of *Quantum Sorcery.* In the intervening 15 years, there have also been tremendous advances and discoveries in the fields of neuroscience and physics that this system proposes as its underpinning. In this time, I have continued to use the techniques described herein as part of my own magical practice. I have also delved deeper into various aspects, by which I have expanded and revised some of the material introduced in prior editions.

When I was a child, I once stated that I wanted to grow up to be either a scientist or a wizard. I have now been studying and practicing diverse forms of magic for 35 years. I am also still an avid student of myriad hard and soft sciences. Apparently, I never did get around to deciding which one I should settle on. This book has opened many doors and created many opportunities for me. It is my sincere hope that it may do the same for you.

This book is dedicated to my muse, CM. Without her encouragement, this work would never have come to be.

I would also like to thank Tau Pneumatikos for her enthusiastic support of my work over the years.

Lastly, RIP Vincent Piazza, seer and necromancer, who placed the needs of others over his own safety in a time of great chaos. Go as you will, my friend.

Io Ion!

Vargr23, Summer Solstice, 2020.

Dave Smith

Introduction

"What is the pattern or the meaning or the why? It does not do harm to the mystery to know a little more about it." - Richard Feynman

Quantum Sorcery is a magical system in which an individual manifests desired effects in the physical world through the exertion of Will. This system makes no supposition regarding the existence or influence of any sort of external agent or higher being as the source of this capability; rather it is based upon the premise that the human mind causes minute changes in the behaviour of subatomic particles and energy. These minute changes, directed by visualisation and focused intent cause a cascade of events to occur, which ultimately result in the manifestation of the desired effect.

Quantum Sorcery incorporates elements from earlier magical systems, as well as physics, mathematics, psychology, and biology. A variety of techniques of open-hand magic, visualisation, and repetition are used that are familiar to many magicians. But in this system such practices are considered to be symbolic devices used for the direct manipulation of reality in the phenomenal world.

In general, I use the term sorcery rather than magic (or magick) to distinguish this system, which considers the Will of the practitioner as the source of the power to manifest change, from systems such as Enochian and Cabbalistic magic which typically assume that the source of power is external to the practitioner. However, as sorcery is a subset of magic, the broader term will also appear throughout the text. I also use the generic term sorcerer to indicate a magician who performs acts of

11

Dave Smith

sorcery regardless of what their gender may be.

The origin of this project arose from a simple question that I could still not answer to my satisfaction after more than 15 years of practicing magic: *What is the underlying mechanism by which the will causes physical change in the universe?* In other words, given my belief that magic works, *how* does it work?

Ultimately, I believe that the power to perform magic comes from within the human mind itself. Still, I could not explain how to bridge the gap between intense desire and actual results. As I investigated this puzzle, I began to find that more often the most pertinent materials were not books about sorcery, but about hard sciences such as physics and neuroscience, or social sciences such as psychology, linguistics, and semiotics. It has been said that magic is simply science that has yet to be explained, but I have come to believe that magic can be more accurately thought of as a natural extension and progression of science. Considering the etymology behind each of the words shows that science is the discipline of observation and knowledge. In contrast, magic is the discipline of influence and prediction. It is my belief that the two are more closely related than most adherents of either are usually willing to acknowledge.

Many religions and magical systems with vastly differing methods and dogma seem capable of achieving the result of exerting Will to cause change, whether the process is referred to as prayer or spell craft. This would seem to indicate that there is not a particular external force which makes these results possible, or if there is, then it is a force which is universally available to all who seek to employ it, rather than being a particular deity who only rewards those who follow a prescribed spiritual path. When the assumption of an outside agent bestowing this capability is removed, the human mind must then be considered as a likely source of this power.

The principle that convinced me of this is known as Occam's Razor. William of Occam, a 14th century logician and Franciscan friar, wrote: *Pluralitas non est ponenda sine necessitate.* Which translates as "Plurality should not be posited without necessity". I apply this to mean that the explanation for a phenomenon which requires the fewest assumptions to be made is most likely to be correct. In this framework, I theorize that within a physical universe, composed of matter and energy, any force capable of manifesting an observable effect on this matter and energy must be a phenomenon originating within that physical universe, rather than external to it. More plainly stated there is no need to ascribe miraculous or supernatural effects to an outside agent when they can be explained as originating from within the person or persons who desire these effects to be manifest.

This book has three sections. The first, *Fundamentals of Sorcery*, provides historical background material on the practice of sorcery from the foundations of the classical world through the 21st century inheritors of this tradition. This is followed by an enumeration of some practical considerations in the practice of sorcery, including instructions on developing a personal symbol set which we'll use in later workings, as well as methods for dealing with the psychic censor, the inner voice of nagging doubt and distraction that inhibits the successful practice of magic.

The second section, *Models of Physical Reality*, resembles a science (or perhaps pseudo-science) text more than a handbook of sorcery. In these chapters, I provide a foundation for understanding the terminology of quantum mechanics, its principles and forces, and the attempts by physicists to construct a unified theory to reconcile their myriad discoveries.

Next, I investigate more radical theories of matter, such as the possibility that the universe and everything in it might be nothing more than a complex hologram, and the possibility that every choice made channels the decision maker into one of the nearly infinite number of different universes. In this section I also investigate chaos theory, the mathematics of hidden patterns and relationships. This discipline is vital to the concept of quantum sorcery regardless of which physical model is found to be the most useful, for it describes the vast effects which can be caused through the application of even minute forces at the smallest scale of reality.

The final section, *Models of Mind and Manipulation*, focuses on the workings of the human mind, and the ways in which the mechanics of sorcery can propagate changes constructed in the mind outward into the phenomenal universe. I examine the possible ways in which all these phenomena can be tied together to actually do the work. This includes the possibility that consciousness, like the universe, could be a holographic construct, or that the emission of measurable energy discharges from human beings could provide the required impetus to initiate a cascade of directed Will.

The last chapter in this section combines the principles of prior chapters into suggested practices for constructing a personally developed system of sorcery designed to provide an interface between the underlying forces that have been explored and the physical world. This system relies on techniques of visualisation and projecting intent through the individual symbols which have been developed for this purpose.

Although you can use Quantum Sorcery as a complete system in its own right, it can also be integrated with other traditions as a meta-system in which to frame them. Likewise, it can also be incorporated into even broader magical models. It is a tool of Will and transformation for use by those who are interested not only in the end, but in the means as well.

This work is probably different in its approach than many other books on magic that you may have read. It is concerned more with describing theory than with practice, although there are some examples that exemplify the techniques described herein. This is no cookbook of incantations. This is intentional. My purpose is to provide you with a new paradigm in which to carry out your magical workings. I am not prescribing a dogmatic system here, rather exploring the underpinnings of the Universe that facilitate the realisation of any magic performed. The sources of all materials are cited, so that you may read them yourself and see if you draw the same conclusions that I have.

Dave Smith

Fundamentals of Sorcery

Dave Smith

Chapter 1
A Chronology of Sorcery

Sorcery breaks no law of nature because there is no Natural Law.

– Hakim Bey

Although there is a great deal of science in this paradigm, this book is about sorcery. This is a term that most people have probably heard before but might not know exactly what it means. The word *sorcery* dates to approximately 1300 C.E. and comes into the English language via the Old French word *sorcerie*. From the Latin words, *sors* (lots), and *legere* (to read) also comes the term *sortilege*, which is the practice of divining the future by reading lots. Associated with this term is the Vulgar Latin **sortiarius* meaning "one who influences fate or fortune." It's interesting that even back to the origins of these words that the act of divining the future is inextricably intertwined with the act of influencing it. As I will explore later, the act of observation is similarly important to the determination of physical reality in real-time as well.

While this definition is a good start, I feel that it is not quite complete. Among the contemporary definitions that I have encountered, I feel the best attempt comes from Ontological Anarchist Hakim Bey. In his collection *T. A. Z. - The Temporary Autonomous Zone*, Bey describes sorcery as "the systematic cultivation of enhanced consciousness or non-ordinary awareness & its deployment in the world of deeds & objects to bring about desired results." He further states that sorcery "involves the manipulation of symbols (which are also things) & of people (who are also symbolic") (Bey, 1985). This definition encapsulates the original, but also expands it in a way that alludes to a greater depth of meaning.

Sorcery as a practice pre-dates recorded history. Paradoxically, it is both the common magic of the tribal witchdoctor, and the closely held secret of medieval mages. It is a pragmatic form of magic, in the most literal sense, which is employed for *doing* and *changing* things. One of its core components is *sympathetic magic*, which has been employed for millennia in the form of rituals designed to ensure good hunting, fertility, and ample rainfall for bountiful harvests. The oldest cave paintings found, which depict hunting scenes, are more than 40,000 years old. At that time, there was no separation between magic and religion. All matters of the numinous world were intertwined. Gods and spirits lived in the sky, the waters, and the earth. Not just successful magic, but sustained life required the cultivation of these entities as allies.

Many people are already familiar with sympathetic magic, although they may not recognize it as such. For example, if I create a small cloth doll that looks like you, and then do everything that I can to imbue it with your properties, such as filling it with bits of your hair and nail clippings, calling it by your name, etc., it then becomes a proxy for you. If I were to do something nasty to this doll, such as stick pins in it, then you would feel the pain. Likewise, if I surround this poppet with emblems of wealth and prosperity, then wealth and prosperity will gather to the real you. Unfortunately, most people are likely more familiar with the first, harmful, example than the second. The fact that

"Voodoo doll kits" can be bought at mainstream bookstores illustrates that the acceptance of this principle is so universal that it has become commonplace and even kitschy. Ironically, the use of dolls in Voodoo practices is largely for positive purposes, whereas pricking or pinning the doll is a largely European practice.

A wealth of material exists from the 16th through the 18th centuries on the practice of sorcery, as it was condemned side by side during that period with accounts of witchcraft and devil worship. One treatise, dating to 1587 states:

> *A Witch is one that worketh by the Devill, or by some develish or curious art, either hurting or healing, revealing things secrete, or foretelling thinges to come, which the devil hath devised to entangle and snare mens soules withal unto damnation. The conjurer, the enchaunter, the sorcerer, the diviner, and whatsoever other sort there is, are indeed compassed within this circle (Gifford, 1587).*

A later work dating to 1727 attempts to describe how these works were performed: "They acted certainly from the Beginning, by certain Mystick or concealed Conjurations, such as uncouth Noises and Sounds, strange Gestures, Postures, and barbarous Magic Noises (Defoe, 1727)."

As anyone who is familiar with contemporary magical practices can tell, not a lot has changed. Sounds, gestures, and postures are still vital components to many forms of magic, and some sorcerers still *invoke* (cause to be manifest internally to the summoner) or *evoke* (cause to be manifest externally to the summoner) what many people would probably consider to be evil spirits. This is not to say that everyone who works magic is interested in such workings, nor that those who do such workings believe that the entities that they are

Dave Smith

transacting with are literally evil spirits.

Many believe that these entities are simply *thought forms*
(pseudo-autonomous psychic entities Willed into
existence by the magician) or personified inner demons.
Some magicians however do seek to transact with entities
that some might perceive as diabolical or malevolent, but
these labels are subjective, and are merely projections of a
culture steeped in an artificially imposed dualistic
worldview in which history has been written by the
victors. Some of these entities may come from lists of
names contained in grimoires dating back hundreds, or in
some cases even thousands of years, whereas others may
come from more modern magical works, or even from
popular horror fiction. It all depends on the desires and
beliefs of the practitioner.

Due to the efforts of many dedicated enthusiasts, many
manuscripts whose ownership in the 17th century might
well have condemned a sorcerer to death can now be
bought online, or even downloaded in their entirety for
free. Some of these works have been modified or
expurgated as they have been passed down from their
original forms, through various translations and
interpretations. Others have remained unchanged for
more than a thousand years. One of these is a semi-
legendary source which has had a profound influence on
sorcery, alchemy, and perhaps even cosmology. It is
known as the *Tabula Smaragdina* or, the *Emerald Tablet of
Hermes Trismegistus*.

The Emerald Tablet of Hermes Trismegistus

The Emerald Tablet of Hermes Trismegistus has been an
object of inspiration and study to alchemists, philosophers,
and sorcerers for over a thousand years, and if there is any

truth to the legends that surround it, perhaps for far longer. I feel that a survey of sorcery would be incomplete if it failed to acknowledge the importance of this document and its author to the Western occult tradition.

Hermes Trismegistus, or Hermes the Thrice Great, who allegedly authored the tablet, was a foundational figure in alchemy. He was renowned for his knowledge of magic, medicine, astrology, and many other disciplines (Hall, 1928). His importance is demonstrated by the usage of the term *Hermetic* to describe various processes relating to alchemy and the occult sciences. His name is a Greek construct which arose when Tehuti (Thoth), the creator god of the Egyptian pantheon, was adopted into the Greek pantheon. Egyptian scribes would often append the epithet *Ao, Ao, Ao,* or "Great, Great, Great" to Tehuti's name in order to indicate his majesty, so the Greeks likewise appended this to the name of their equivalent deity, Hermes.

In addition to the Emerald Tablet, Hermes Trismegistus was also the purported author of the *Corpus Hermeticum*, a collection of Hellenic Gnostic texts, as well as the *Divine Pymander*, which is the earliest of the Hermetic texts. However, it was common in Egyptian magical practice for individual magicians to self-identify with the god and adopt his name for their endeavours to lend them gravitas. For this reason, it is likely that the body of writings attributed to him, which comprises more than thirty thousand manuscripts, is the work of numerous anonymous individuals (Holmstrom, 1998, Hall).

The origin of the physical Tablet itself is unknown. Stories say that it was made of translucent green stone or glass, with the text similar to Phoenician characters appearing as a bas relief rather than an engraving. This implies that it may have been cast. Numerous legends surround the Tablet, its creation, and the identities of its various owners. One legend states that it was an antediluvian artifact created by Thoth, a priest-king of Atlantis, in order to insure that Atlantean wisdom was preserved despite the impending destruction of that continent. The Tablet was supposedly found concealed in a sacred pillar hidden near Thebes during a search initiated by the Pharaoh Amenhotep IV, who is better known now by the name he later adopted, Akhenaten.

This legend further states that almost 1000 years after Akhenaten's death, the Tablet was found in the Great Pyramid of Giza by soldiers in service to Alexander the Great. Alexander had long sought the tablet, and once attained, he displayed it in the great library in the city of Alexandria. Upon Alexander's death, the location of the Tablet was lost. It was discovered hidden in a cave by a Syrian named Balinas, who became better known by his Greek name, Apollonius of Tyana, as a philosopher, alchemist, and Neo-Pythagorean mystic. Perhaps it is fitting that the legends mention Alexander, as the investigation of this topic has been comparable to unravelling a Gordian knot of misinformation, disinformation, and wild speculation.

Although no credible record exists of the original Tablet's supposed final resting place, there is also no account of its destruction. In all honesty, such a physical artifact as a literal green glass tablet likely never have existed at all as such (Seligmann, 1948). In his mention of the Tablet in his seminal work *The Secret Teachings of all Ages*, Manly P Hall (1928) notes that "Authorities do not agree as to the genuineness of this Table, some declaring it to be a post-Christian fraud, but there is much evidence that, regardless of its author, the Table is of great antiquity." In the absence of the physical artifact, its text, which was widely copied and disseminated by Alexandrian scribes, has come to be known by the Tablet's name.

Regardless of where or when the Tablet originated, the text that it contained can be found in another text that dates back to the eighth century C.E. in a work titled *Kitab al-Asrar*, or *The Book of Secrets* by Abu Bakr Muhammad ibn Zakariya Al-Razi (864-930 C.E.). It was then translated into Latin as *Liber Secretorum Alchimie* by Constantine of Pisa in 1257 C.E. Earlier but fragmentary portions of the Tablet's contents are also said to be found in older sources, such as the Leyden Papyrus, which dates to the third century C.E. (Seligmann). The following is one translation of the Tablet's text:

> *The truth, certainty, truest, without untruth. What is above is like what is below. What is below is like what is above. The miracle of unity is to be attained. Everything is formed from the contemplation of unity, and all things come about from unity, by means of adaptation. Its parents are the Sun and Moon. It was borne by the wind and nurtured by the Earth. Every wonder is from It and its power is complete. Throw it upon earth, and earth will separate from fire. The impalpable separated from the palpable. Through wisdom it rises slowly from the world to heaven. Then it descends to the world combining the power of the upper and the lower. Thus you will have the illumination of all the world and darkness will disappear. This is the power of all strength- it overcomes that which is delicate and penetrates through solids. This was the means of the creation of the world. And in the future wonderful developments will be made, and this is the way. I am Hermes the Threefold Sage, so named because I hold the three elements of all wisdom. And thus ends the revelation of the work of the Sun (Shah, 1964).*

Whether the Tablet is thought to be the product of gods or of men is ultimately irrelevant, compared to the importance of its message. What is above is like what is below. What is below is like what is above. These simple statements summarize the principle of the macrocosm and the microcosm, which is in turn the foundation of sorcery itself.

The term macrocosm comes from the Greek words *macros*, large, and *kosmos*, world. Conversely, microcosm is the complementary term meaning small (*mikros*) world. The principle that arises from this passage is that if a change is caused on a small scale, such as on a model or on some small portion of a large system that the effect also manifests in the large system. The reverse is also true from the standpoint that small phenomena are representative of large phenomena. This principle is often expressed through the belief that man is a microcosmic representation of some celestial creator. Although the concepts behind this idea were essential to several mystery schools of the fifth century B.C.E., such as those of Democritus and Pythagoras, it is through the translated Arabic works containing the principles of the Tablet that such ideas were revived and introduced into the sphere of European alchemy and sorcery.

As in modern times, it was a common practice in the ancient world to incorporate older magical texts into new compendiums. Since this leads to errors in translation and attribution, the ultimate source of the principles contained in the Emerald Tablet will likely never be known. Fortunately, this does not reduce the importance of the text as a means of memetic transmission. These ideas are still as applicable to magical practice today as they were when they were first set down.

Although the Emerald Tablet and other works attributed to Hermes Trismegistus were most esteemed among alchemists, their influence upon other forms of magical practice is easily seen. Unfortunately, despite its shared ancestry with more structured and "respectable" magical forms, the practice of sorcery still has its share of detractors, not only among the pious, but even among those who practice magic themselves. *In Dogme et Rituel de la Haute Magie*, nineteenth-century magician Eliphas Levi (1896) wrote:

> *The magician avails himself of a force which he knows, the sorcerer seeks to misuse that which he does not understand... The magician is the sovereign pontiff of Nature, the sorcerer is her profaner only. The sorcerer is in the same relation to the magician that a superstitious and fanatical person bears to a truly religious man.*

Contemporary Sorcery: What's so Low About Low Magic?

In discussions of contemporary magical practices, sorcery is often spoken of in a derogatory manner. In contrast to ceremonial or "high" magic, sorcery is often termed "low magic", or as one author calls it, "mundane black magic" (Nicht, 2001). The contrasting forms are also referred to as *Theurgy* (from the Greek for "god-working") and *Thaumaturgy* (from "wonder-working"). Theurgy was also contrasted against *Goetia*, from the ancient Greek word meaning sorcery. Regarding the difference between the two, Heinrich Cornelius Agrippa wrote:

> *Now the parts of ceremonial magic are goetia and theurgia. Goetia is unfortunate, by the commerces of unclean spirits made up of the rites of wicked curiosities, unawful charms, and deprecations, and is*

Dave Smith

abandoned and execrated by all laws (Tyson, 1992).

What ultimately distinguishes between and high and low magic? The answer is not entirely intuitive and is in some ways quite arbitrary. Although there is no universal definition as to exactly what magic itself is, Aleister Crowley provided a concise definition that has been frequently cited, analysed, and repeated. Crowley (1929) wrote that: "Magick is the Science and Art of causing Change to occur in conformity with Will".

This is an encompassing statement that many practitioners of widely diverse magical traditions can hopefully agree upon. However, from this common ground, there are likely as many ways to classify magical workings as there are magicians. From a sampling of the myriad sources available, I will try to construct a general description of how others have classified them, and then I will present the case that such classifications are ultimately irrelevant.

Most systems attempt to classify magic based on what purpose it is used for, and in what way it is accomplished. In broad terms, high magic seeks to refine the self in order to bring it into greater accord with a perceived divinity. Low magic is more concerned with altering earthly circumstances for the benefit of a sorcerer or the detriment of their adversaries. In a testament to the human love of opposing dualities, this contrast is often expressed in terms of "White" or "Black" magic. This questionable dichotomy is distinct from the frequent categorization of certain types of magic as inherently feminine, such as *Seidh*, and others such as *Galdr*, as masculine, and thus superior in historical reckoning.

In contemporary reckoning, magic is generally referred to as White if the purpose of working it is to achieve a connection to the magician's *Holy Guardian Angel*. This supposed angel is considered by some, including myself, to be an allegory of the higher Self. Others believe that it is literally a divine messenger sent from some etheric paradise. This magic ostensibly seeks to uplift the human spirit into the realm of the divine, and is frequently, although not always, couched in the symbolism of the God of Abraham, JHVH. As such, this type of magic generally presupposes that there are external, incarnate deities which may be contacted or petitioned by the magician. This type of magic is also referred to by some as the *Right-Hand Path*.

At the opposite end of the modern magical spectrum, but still frequently structured and dogmatic, is so-called Black magic. This form is typically assumed to utilize "evil" spirits, demons, or other denizens of the netherworld, as well as names and symbols contained in the grimoires and manuscripts previously mentioned. These entities are brought forth and commanded to do the bidding of their summoner, which can include such tasks as imparting information, influencing events, or sowing misfortune on their master's behalf.

Collectively, both "low" sorcery and "high" goetia are often lumped together and referred to as the *Left-Hand Path*. In addition to various other earthly matters, this category of magic is also concerned with the subjugation of the Will of another. Ironically, the archetypal "love spell" falls within this category.

In some limited views, regardless of considerations of high or low magic, there is only black and white, with nothing in between. This is a severely limited point of view. Other methods of classification acknowledge that like almost everything else, magic is a continuum that cannot be so easily categorized. These more comprehensive systems include yet a third category, Grey magic. As the name implies, this is neither white nor black. This form of magic is used to benefit the magician rather than to uplift his or her spirit to the divine realms, without the implied use of evil entities or actions. One author has also proposed the term *Off-White* for this style of magic (Carroll, 1995).

Within this tripartite system of classification, I propose that most of the intentions and workings in traditional sorcery would fall largely within the confines of Grey magic, with occasional forays into the "black" end of the continuum. There is no inherent law of retribution to be found in most forms of sorcery. The exact nature of sorcerous work, in terms of good and evil, and right and wrong are left up to the ethics of the individual sorcerer. The belief that "what goes around comes around" is already entrenched in a great many systems of human culture and socialization, so there is no need for the universe to keep score as to who has been naughty or nice.

The designation of any magical system as either white or black also presupposes the acceptance of the idea that some acts and thoughts are inherently good or evil. This is an overly simplistic viewpoint. All activities within the realm of human experience are relative to the cultures and situations which contain them, although some practices have attained forbidden status across enough cultures as to appear nearly universal.

Every person who chooses to take up the practice of sorcery must make their own decisions as to what constitutes appropriate behaviour for them, in their circumstances, in any given moment. Those who cannot bear the thought of such responsibility might want to reconsider engaging in the practice, for with it comes the realisation that every mind has within it the capability to contemplate the full gamut of actions, from the atrocious to the sublime.

The only entity to whom you are ultimately answerable, metaphysically speaking, is yourself. Learn and employ what techniques you will and use them as you see fit. Do not work your sorcery based on the bias or judgement of any other worker of Will, be they theurge or thaumaturge, nor in fear of damnation by higher powers. Your path is yours alone, and you are the highest power.

Even though sorcery is typically regarded as a lesser form of magic compared to its ceremonial counterparts, its practice has persisted into the modern era. Through the works of several 20th century authors and explorers, forms of it have emerged as practical systems of magical working in the West. One of the foremost of these authors was English artist and magician Austin Osman Spare.

Austin Osman Spare

Austin Osman Spare was if nothing else, an unapologetic sorcerer. He felt that faith and religion had no place in magic, and his dislike of ceremonial magicians was intense. Regarding the latter, he wrote:

> *These Magicians, whose insincerity is their safety, are but the unemployed dandies of the Brothels... Their practices prove their incapacity; they have no magic to intensify the normal, the joy of a child or healthy person, none to evoke their pleasure or wisdom from themselves (Spare, 1913).*

Spare conceived of a transcendental primal force which he named *Kia*. Like the Tao, he wrote: "The Kia which can be expressed by conceivable ideas, is not the eternal Kia,

31

which burns up all belief but is the archetype of 'self,' the slavery of mortality." To unlock the power of this Kia, Spare created a magical system which used *sigils*, or "sacred letters" as he called them, which are statements of desire distilled into symbols for transmission to the subconscious mind by combining the letters of the statement into a non-linguistic symbol. He energized these sigils through the use of ecstatic states achieved by hyperventilation (via his Death Posture) and orgasm. Through this state of vacuity, which he termed "Neither-Neither", he stated that the "capability to attempt the impossible becomes known…"

Spare produced a number of written works in addition to his paintings, but as he demonstrated in *Anathema of Zos,* in 1924, he eventually became disillusioned with his contemporaries, and withdrew into relative seclusion. It was not until 1948 that he began writing for public consumption again (Hawkins, 1996). Spare died in 1956, leaving his unpublished papers to his friend Kenneth Grant. For several decades, Spare's ideas on sorcery remained largely dormant. It was not until the late 1970's, after Grant's publishing of Spare's material that the current he had begun would resurge again through the efforts of a small group of English sorcerers.

Chaos Magick Emerges

In November 1974, several London magicians began meeting in a group that revolved around the Sorcerer's Apprentice bookstore. This group came to be called the Stoke Newington Sorcerers. Among them were a number of young occultists whose names are now well-know, including Peter Carroll, Ray Sherwin, Gerald Suster, and Charles Brewster. Through Kenneth Grant's books, Carroll became interested in the works of the early 20th century artist and sorcerer Austin Osman Spare. Carroll, along with Ray Sherwin, were inspired by Spare's techniques. They desired to create a new type of magic that was less bound to the dogmatic and stale techniques of the general western magical corpus. Their creation was known as Chaos Magick. Ray Sherwin (2015) explained the origin of the name:

> *We formulated the term 'Chaos Magick' to indicate the randomness of the universe and the individual's relationship with it. The antithesis of chaos, cosmos, is the universe suitably defined by the successful magician for his own purposes and that definition is under constant scrutiny and may be regularly changed. Chaos is expressive of this philosophy and reinforces the idea that there is no permanent model for the individual's relationship with everything that he is not.*

Through his writings, which were later published as the book *Liber Null,* Carroll presented a magical system independent of dogma and encouraged the use of whatever symbolic means most appealed to the magician. Sherwin's own *Book of Results* further expanded this novel approach to magical working. They also spawned a new magical order, *The Illuminates of Thanateros.* In the introduction to *Liber Null,* Carroll (1987) states that "The Illuminates of Thanateros are the magical heirs to the Zos Kia Cultus and the A.A."

One aspect of this new system involved the re-visitation and clarification of Spare's techniques of sigilization. Although the details of this period of magical revival are too expansive a topic to cover here in depth, it is well-documented by many of the participants themselves, although often in conflicting accounts.

Dave Smith

Chaos Magick is a free-form magical paradigm which is practiced in as many ways as there are magicians who employ it. The adoption of temporary belief structures, the use of mathematical formulas in rituals, and the creation and empowerment of thought forms or *servitors* to perform desired tasks are several of the more commonly encountered ideas in this system. In later years, additional aspects such as the invocation of pop culture icons and the inclusion of horror fiction pantheons as usable godforms have also been included under the aegis of this type of magic.

Like classical sorcery, Chaos Magick focuses on achieving desired results rather than following a proscribed method for achieving them. The phrases "Fake it 'til you make it", and "Nothing is true, everything is permitted" are representative of its tenets. Practitioners of other forms of magic, particularly those who favor a great deal of hierarchy and structure have frequently attacked the validity of Chaos Magick and its advocates, but its persistence indicates that it does work and produces results for its users.

One commenter declared in 1988 that the Chaos current was officially dead (Biraco, 2002). This declaration seems to have been premature. Chaos Magick didn't die, it simply changed from being the practice of a few small groups and isolated individuals to being a more widespread and divergent practice distributed over a far wider area. Such is the life cycle of any underground movement. Too, many of the foundational practitioners of Chaos Magick became Balkanized into mutually loathing factions and have continued to feud with one another for over three decades. Whatever one of them writes or opines is often piled on by their adversaries.

The growth of the Internet facilitated greater communication among magicians in widely dispersed geographic areas, which helped to expand the body of works in Chaos Magick. In the mid-1990's, distributed networks of magicians, such as the *Z(Cluster)* coordinated online rituals which spanned continents, and magical working groups formed with members never meeting face-to-face. The *DKMU* carried the current in a similar vein into the 21st century. The adaptive principles of Chaos Magick have become ideally suited to this medium. Some magicians have explored the relationship between computers and magic to an advanced degree, even constructing programs which are designed to be spells in their own right.

Summary

Sorcery is a magical system which relies on the attainment of altered states and the manipulation of symbols to achieve desired results. It encompasses the use of sympathetic magic, which is the belief that larger systems or entities can be influenced by performing actions on a smaller simulacrum. This principle is reflected in the writings of the pseudo-legendary Hermes Trismegistus contained on the fabled Emerald Tablet which is summarized as "What is above is like what is below. What is below is like what is above."

Although disparaged by many ceremonial magicians, and condemned as black magic by the church, sorcery has progressed over time from a secretive and socially dangerous activity into a far more mainstream practice. The increasing rate at which information has become available to those who seek it, whether through printed materials or via electronic means has contributed greatly to this phenomenon, as has wider societal acceptance of non-dogmatic belief systems.

The works of Austin Osman Spare were inspirational to the creation of Chaos Magick as the contemporary manifestation of many of the concepts which originated in classical sorcery. Despite being declared dead, Chaos Magick has continued to adapt and evolve into a far wider phenomenon, branching like a hydra into myriad forms, embracing and co-opting technology and pop culture as mediums of manifestation. It persists largely due to the very reasons for which it is criticized: flexibility, adaptation, and the rejection of the concept of ultimate truth.

Chapter 2
Practical Considerations in Sorcery

Belief can structure reality.

– Peter Carroll

Sorcery, like all forms of magic, is a tool. It is not an ideology or a religion. It is a method that gives users the ability to gain some form of control over the phenomenal universe. By this, I mean the perceivable domain of physical matter which can be observed by others, as opposed to the speculative internal reality which is intrinsic to each human mind. Not every magical working produces results that are visible to someone other than the one who performed it, but if no externally perceptible results are *ever* generated, then the activity might more accurately be labelled as creative visualisation or self-programming rather than sorcery. That is not to say that such exercises are not valuable themselves, but they are outside of the scope of this work.

Change does not come casually or easily. It only comes through the combination of intent and intensity. Many people can desire and envision change, but a far smaller number have the Will and awareness to actually externalize their vision and make it manifest. This chapter presents several concepts to help facilitate the development of this ability.

Energy Loss in Magical Operations

It is not enough to understand the principles of magic; nor to believe in the mechanism by which it is performed. One cannot use undisciplined desire alone to change reality to fit their needs. This understanding and Will must still be translated into the desired effects via some practical method Were this not the case, then anyone who wanted could freely alter reality on a whim and a wave, and practices such as alchemy and magic would never have emerged in the first place.

In sorcery as in other magical disciplines, the term *energy* is often used but is seldom well defined. From a physical standpoint, energy is nothing more than the capacity to do work. It is a measure of the capability to change a given system from a starting condition to a desired ending condition. In this case I am using the term to represent the focused intent of the sorcerer. The work that this energy is being applied to do is to achieve the results of a magical operation. In later chapters, I will introduce another form of energy to which the following principles also apply, but for now this abstracted definition will suffice.

In general, there is a direct relationship between the amount of energy invested in a magical operation, and how much that operation can accomplish. Unfortunately, it must be assumed that only a fraction of the total energy invested in producing a desired result will ultimately be brought to bear on the task. If we operate under the assumption that the laws of physics govern the phenomenal universe, as well as assume that magic is performed by affecting energy within this universe, then we can say that these laws must apply to magic as well.

Unfortunately, there is no known process which allows a perfect transfer of energy. Some of it is inevitably lost during transmission and application. A study of the laws of thermodynamics, motion, and mechanical work can provide some insight as to how much energy may be lost before it can be put to use. Not all these laws apply, but there are many analogies that can be made. For example, it is my observation that consensus reality acts as a force of inertia and resistance against causing changes in the system.

In physics, inertia is a property of matter which prescribes that a non-moving object will remain at rest, and a moving object will continue to move in a straight line, unless some external force acts on the object. Correspondingly, consensus reality is a term popularized by philosopher, magician, and humourist Robert Anton Wilson to describe the average reality experienced and reinforced by a given group of people in a specific time and place. The collective consciousness of all other minds in proximity to the sorcerer, even without directed Will, comprises a formidable barrier which must be overcome. In order to manipulate reality, there is some threshold energy which must be exceeded. Narrowing the focus of intent can help overcome this limitation if initial attempts are met with too much resistance.

Counteracting Energy Loss

One of the ways to make additional energy available for when it is needed is to invest it into a physical object. Talismans, amulets, and fetishes are common in many magical systems, and Quantum Sorcery is no different. What *is* different is the way that such objects are believed to function. It is true that these items may be acting simply as a focal point for magical energy, but it may also be that these items function in the same way as batteries and other components do for electrical energy. In this paradigm, a sigil would be conceptualized as something more akin to a capacitor, in that it releases its energy in a short burst, rather than a slower trickle.

From a different standpoint, the build-up of magical energy can also be considered to occur purely within the subconscious of the sorcerer, and that the physical tools and symbols used for ritual are only the triggers to direct its expenditure. This is in effect a trick played on the self, so-called sleight of mind, taking advantage of the adage that belief forms reality in this realm. Within this model, an association is created between the physical object or symbol, and the availability of greater power for the sorcerer's use than could otherwise be wielded. With this understanding, any object or symbol may be employed for magical purposes.

Due to the growth of online commerce, many pieces of occult paraphernalia can now be obtained in areas of the world where these items were formerly difficult or impossible to find. It is true that the appropriate trappings, dress, and props can help create a ritual mind space, but the lack of these things should also not be a cause for limitation or failure. If such items are needed, it is far better to fabricate them oneself if possible. The act of designing and creating a dagger, staff, medallion, or other magical tool creates a stronger connection between the sorcerer and the tool than simply purchasing it. Consequentially, the stronger the personal connection to the tool, the more potent that tool becomes. Failing this, it is better to purchase a hand-made piece of ritual gear or jewellery than one that has been mass-produced. The intent that is placed in such an object by its creator may to some extent be available to the end user.

The process of investing personal energy into a physical object, whether self-made or purchased can be as elaborate or as simple as the sorcerer wishes it to be. If desired, a sorcerer can create elaborate consecration rituals for this purpose, but the simple act of holding an object, breathing on it, or marking it with blood, saliva, or sexual fluid can also suffice. It may help to envision the push as a great wave striking the shore. As the energy rolls towards landfall, the water briefly pulls back into the wave, which then surges forward and breaks, releasing its energy. Certain Tai Chi movements are also analogous to this process.

Manipulating Symbols

Being able to manipulate symbols in all their forms is one of the core components of sorcery. To this end, one of the useful things a sorcerer can do is to create a set of symbols that have personal meaning for use in magical workings. Austin Spare called this system, which he constructed through automatic drawing, *the sacred alphabet*. Although it has become better known as the *Alphabet of Desire*. By creating such an alphabet, the symbols have only the specific meanings which the subconscious mind of the sorcerer attaches to them, and no more. The subconscious mind operates on a symbolic model rather than a linguistic one, and the images that percolate up from it to the conscious mind, if they can be recorded and deciphered, can be used in reverse fashion by the conscious mind to give instructions to the subconscious. This is essentially the same model on which sigils work. Even if designed with active input from the conscious mind, personal symbols become more attuned to the sorcerer than those derived from other sources.

The technique of automatic drawing can be easily learned, although practice helps achieve a consistent level of desired results. Hold a pen to paper as if drawing or writing normally. With eyes closed, take several slow, deep breaths, and allow tension to drain from the body on each exhalation. Allow extraneous thoughts to drain from the mind. When working initially, do not impose any other specific thoughts or focus. Allow the pen to move freely on the paper for as long as desired. When finished, examine the resulting lines, and note any which seem significant. Austin Spare wrote about his own technique:

> *The Hand must be trained to work freely and without control, by practice in making simple forms with a continuous involved line without afterthought, i.e. its intention should just escape consciousness... the mind in a state of oblivion, without desire towards reflection or pursuit of materialistic intellectual suggestions, is in a condition to produce successful drawings of one's personal ideas, symbolic in meaning and wisdom*
> (Spare and Carter, 1916).

Prior to beginning this process, create a list of concepts, emotions, and any other entities you want to represent in the alphabet. Before initiating an automatic drawing session, select one of the items in the list. Meditate on this item and let the subconscious express its associations with the concept. While in this receptive state, start drawing. You will use the lines and shapes generated through this exercise to form the core of the personal letter which represents the selected concept. If a specific image jumps to the conscious mind while in this process, record it adjacent to the results of the automatic drawing. You can then use these flashes of insight to add to the final rendering of the letter. There are no restrictions, apart from imagination and artistic ability, as to how complex or simple each letter should be. Once the alphabet is completed, you can use it as a form of magical shorthand for creating sigils, seals, or any other written magical purposes.

If creating such an alphabet from scratch is not feasible or desired, then an existing set of symbols can be adopted or assembled. Select from an ideographic writing system such as runes, kanji, or hieroglyphs as the basis for the creation of a personal alphabet. This can suffice, but it might be more difficult to connect with than a personal set. I have also found that existing non-magical icons and commonly encountered symbols sometimes lend themselves to adaptation for magical purposes. Note that a personal symbol set need not always consist only of written characters. Some sorcerers consider the set of mudras, repetitive motions, sounds, and even emotional states used during ritual workings to be part of their alphabets.

There are considerations when using previously existing symbols from other magical disciplines. It is both a blessing and a curse that such symbols have well-known and long-established meanings. These meanings are based ultimately on the work of one or a few individuals, then reinforced by the consensus of all who have learned them as rote. This fact can be leveraged to good use, without the necessity of additional interpretation, but it can also be a limiting factor.

Ultimately, using whatever methods to bring more energy and Will to bear on a desire, the greater the chance that the desire will manifest. Intense visualisation of the desired results coming to pass is another way in which this can be accomplished. Don't visualise this situation as being in the future. Embrace it as already occurring in the present, as the way that things already are. Reflect this in attitude and especially in speech. This is an ancient technique, which can be found in Egyptian magical writings, some of which date back to the 2nd century B.C.E (Holmstrom, 1998). The stronger the image that is constructed of the reality desired, the easier it becomes to realise that reality.

A method for adopting this technique that I have personally used is to write future journal entries, which contain references to events that I wish to occur as if they have already come to pass. In this process, I jump ahead a few weeks, months, or even years, and write with conviction about the successes that I have had in various endeavours. This method has also been explored in a far more in-depth manner in the form of personal hyper-fictions created by magician writers such as William S. Burroughs, and more recently Grant Morrison. Attuning the self in as many ways as possible with the reality that is desired to be manifest is essential.

In addition to being a potent magical practice, this method is also a powerful mental exercise. It is one of the techniques described by Maxwell Maltz in his 1960 book *Psycho-Cybernetics*. The underlying idea is that you continually envision a successful situation, constantly adding nuance and detail until this simulacrum manifests as your reality.

It is no accident that consensus reality stands in the way of the manifestation of personal Will. As individuals mature within a culture, they are expected to subscribe to, and in fact assist in the reinforcement of, the consensus reality of that culture. This generally includes accepting the dominant spiritual paradigm. Failure to participate as expected can result in sanctions such as shunning, imprisonment, or even death in the most extreme of cases. The acceptance of external definitions of what constitutes the difference between real and unreal contribute to the creation and reinforcement of what Peter Carroll refers to as the *psychic censor* (Carroll, 1987).

The Psychic Censor and How to Thwart It

The psychic censor is a mechanism of the conscious mind which determines, based on rules which have been internalized from external sources, what limits are placed on possibility. In general, the psychic censor tells the conscious mind that magic is a fallacy, and that the power of the mind is insufficient to cause actual change in the universe. It also acts as a filter which limits sensory (and extra-sensory) input. As much of a hindrance to the practice of magic that this construct sounds, it is also necessary. Without this filtering mechanism, it would be difficult, if not impossible, to function in the world on a daily basis, as the conscious mind would be overwhelmed by the sheer volume of input to which it would be exposed. As H. P. Lovecraft alluded, this censor also protects mankind from the shrieking horror of realising how miniscule and imperilled our place in the universe is.

Fortunately, there are several ways by which the censor can be overcome on a temporary or limited basis, without permanently impairing its functionality. One of these methods, and probably the most frequently employed, is to ascribe the source of magical power to a higher being, such as a god or demon. This placates the censor by inactivating the self as the causal agent in an act of Will. The request for the desired result is passed to the supposed higher entity via prayer or evocation. Unfortunately, this method is logically fallible, as it requires an even greater suspension of disbelief, and the adoption of a larger complex of assumptions than simply accepting that the self is capable of direct action. This path is unfortunately a trap which places limitations on the personal power of a sorcerer. Because of this, I do not recommend its use unless you have a firm grasp on yourself and are simply using this belief system as a tool via paradigm adoption.

Another way to suppress and avoid the psychic censor's scrutiny is to allow the desire for change to be passed off from the conscious mind to the subconscious. Many sorcerers rely on methods such as sigilisation, glossolalia (the vocalization of nonsensical sounds and phrases), or other methods which compress the linguistic construction of the desire into a symbolic form which can be better actualized by the subconscious mind. This method is generally effective but relies on the concept of avoiding a lust for results. If the sorcerer is unable to expunge the desire from the conscious mind, then the psychic censor can be activated, and will sabotage the desire with disbelief, guilt, or other undesired processes.

I propose that rather than trying to work around the psychic censor, there is a greater benefit in conditioning it through various methods, so that it accepts a greater range of possibilities, and no longer inhibits belief in the self's ability to cause changes to phenomenal reality, yet still fulfils its necessary role as a throttle and filter between the self and the phenomenal world. Such an endeavour should not be undertaken lightly, for there are risks involved in altering one's personal reality construct. There is no foil sticker on the subconscious mind which states "Warranty void if seal is broken," but it is a good idea to act as if there is unless you know well what you are doing in there. The goal in this conditioning is to allow the self a greater degree of freedom, without losing grip on consensus reality.

Why does this matter? For good or ill, most sorcerers, myself included, must still be able to successfully interact with the real world at large, regardless of what our opinions on it may be. Remember that when the ritual is over, and the circle is dispelled that the *Magister Templi* still probably must pump their own gasoline and take out their garbage. As I discuss later, the practice of sorcery already necessitates at least some degree of egotism, but lapsing into solipsism, or the belief that the self is the only reality, is a trap that must be avoided. Such a point of view is interesting as an exercise, but the neuroses, paranoia, and megalomania which can accompany it will probably provide few benefits.

There are several ways in which the psychic censor can be conditioned. Some of these involve a greater degree of risk than others. Several methods, such as self-hypnosis and meditation rely on some form of conscious conditioning, continually repeated with the intent that such behaviour will over time reshape the process of the censor. Another possible method is loosely based on the theory of memetics.

Far more than simply funny images on the web, memes are analogous to genes, and are the replicators of cultural imitation and information. The concept of memes was first proposed by biologist Richard Dawkins but has been further explored and expanded by others such as Susan Blackmore (Dawkins, 1976). Memes are comprised of both conscious and subconscious components, and thus they are capable of effectively bridging the gap between these parts of the mind as part of their very nature. The concept of the psychic censor seems based upon the assumption that an implanted thought process cannot pass harmoniously between the two segments of the mind without interference, and that the conscious ego will hamper the functionality of the thought becoming reality.

Memes can counteract this effect by acting as tunnels which allow conscious thoughts to reinforce implanted subconscious programs. Consider the meme "Dogmatic Faith" for example. A mind that is infected by this meme will have numerous patterns of behaviour that are implanted in each segment of the mind. Each such aspect serves to validate and reinforce patterns present in the other to facilitate a greater degree of acceptance of the message of conformity, obedience, and homogeneity of thought. Before the victim knows it, their Will is no longer their own.

To take advantage of this method of conditioning, create a self-directed set of sensory components including sounds, visual images, etc. as triggers which are directed at encoding a statement of Will. "I will discard my preconceived notions regarding the structure of reality" would be an example of such a statement. Repeated encounters with the trigger images, sounds, or phrases associated with this statement of intent can cause the idea to eventually penetrate the subconscious mind. Skilled advertisers rely on this technique extensively. Why let them have all the fun?

By strict definition, the informational packet created by this method is not actually a meme, unless the sorcerer chooses to disseminate the idea to others, but the process by which the mind accepts the message will be very similar. This method may seem odd, but it can work very effectively. It is an advertising campaign designed to sell the idea of power *over* the self *to* the self. If feasible, this campaign can be opened up for exposure to others as well so that their collective intent contributes to the operation. There are various online forums that are ripe for garnering attention onto one's memetic creations.

Some of the most potent methods for overcoming the censor are also potentially the riskiest. These include the techniques investigated by researchers such as Dr. John Lilly and Terence McKenna which employ psychotropic substances, such as LSD or psilocybin mushrooms to expand the mind and embrace alternate paradigms which remain even after the experience has ended. Lilly referred to this process as *metaprogramming* (Lilly, 1972). He theorized that the human mind is a biocomputer, and thus that human beings are programmable entities. He sought to create a "metaprogramming language" by which a person could better refine and control their own metaprograms, and hence gain a greater degree of control over both their conscious and subconscious processes. He performed a series of experiments in which he would adopt a set of "Basic Beliefs", ingest LSD, and then attempt to determine what level of intensity of those Beliefs he could achieve.

Terence McKenna also investigated the possibility of removing the barrier between what he terms the ego and the *Overself* (McKenna, 1984). Unlike Lilly, his experiments were done using naturally occurring sources of tryptamine, such as the psilocybin mushroom and ayahuasca, a psychoactive preparation of the Amazonian vine *Banisteriopsis caapi*. Experimentation with this technique is obviously not recommended for novices. McKenna (1990) himself states:

> *Naturally, whenever a compound is introduced into the body, one must exercise caution and be well informed with regard to possible side effects. Professional psychedelic investigators are aware of these factors and freely acknowledge that the obligation to be well informed is of primary importance.*

I have no doubt that many otherwise open-minded people recoil at the thought of using psychotropic substances as a means to modify their personal parameters of reality.

As technologist and psychonaut Mark Pesce observed, "Shortcuts to gnosis invariably draw the ire of those who have tirelessly sacrificed to receive the same benefits as those bestowed by pineal grace" (Pesce, 2000). While I am neither advocating nor condemning this practice, dismissing any method which has the capability to expand personal consciousness should not be done without consideration. Ultimately everyone must rely on their own best judgment, weighing awareness of personal limitations and willingness to engage in activities deemed unlawful by civic authorities before reaching an informed decision.

The degree to which any of these techniques or combinations are effective in conditioning the subconscious mind varies based on several factors. Quite simply, some people have an easier time changing their behaviour patterns, belief structures, and subconscious programming than others. A brutally honest self-assessment of personal beliefs, attitude, and limitations may be the best way to begin such a process. What do you, at this moment, genuinely believe about the nature of existence? Do you believe in a higher spiritual power of any kind? In contrast, do you find such a possibility to be ridiculous? Are you a fatalist? Do you believe in free-will? Angels? Ghosts? Elves? All these questions are just a beginning. Once you have a firm grasp on where you are, you can formulate a plan to convey you to where you wish to be.

While any of the above methods of relaxing the psychic censor may be employed in quantum sorcery, this system also relies on an awareness and acceptance of the principles of quantum mechanics and chaos theory to facilitate its workings. This is accomplished by understanding that at a subatomic level, physical reality itself is reduced to a field of probabilities which can be manipulated by introducing minute changes in the trajectory of subatomic particles. These infinitesimal influences will propagate to cause far greater physical effects in the phenomenal universe.

Reducing the scale at which an influence needs to be applied in order to produce desired results further helps to convince the conscious mind that such ends are attainable. This takes advantage of the dogmatic instruction of scientific principles common in Western educational systems, as well as the reduced subconscious resistance to incorporating new components which fall within the realm of science which is instilled by such education. Whether or not the mechanism by which magic causes change is actually related to these theories is immaterial. It is the *possibility* that these principles are the causal force which frees the mind to believe that they *are* the cause. These theories and their implications will be introduced and discussed in subsequent chapters.

The Egotism of Sorcery

There is an inherent degree of egotism necessary to practice sorcery. Not only must a person sincerely believe that they have the capability to alter reality by exerting Will upon it, but they must also seize this prerogative and actually *do it*. Reading makes you a scholar. Doing magic makes you a magician. Such temerity flies in the face of social conventions, as well as any religious faith which espouses the belief that everything in existence is part of some deity's grand plan. It is this willingness to venture outside of the boundaries of consensus reality, and to strive for personal actualization which causes sorcerers to be labelled, and in some times and places condemned to death, as heretics, lunatics, or diabolists.

To be a sorcerer is to be outside the boundaries of society, while still being constrained to follow its rules when interacting with it. As I touched on briefly before, society thrives on homogeneity, and gives only limited leeway to those who flaunt its rules and disregard its hierarchies. Workers of Will are not generally welcome among common folk. Consider that there is a reason that in earlier cultures the wise woman's hut is usually on the edge of the village, if not just outside of it. Likewise, in fairy tales wizards always live in distant towers, not on the main drag. In the contemporary world where the opinions and recommendations of a single authority figure, such as a law enforcement officer or psychotherapist, can have profound and lifelong effects upon the freedom and rights of an individual, there is much to be gained by learning how to function incognito when necessary.

This is not to say that a sorcerer must live a life of fear and concealment. Nor does this mean that freedom of expression or personal style must be suppressed. What it does mean is that a profound awareness of society at large should be cultivated, as well as an understanding of just how far of a deviation from the norm will be tolerated within it before someone is labelled a threat. Power can be used to radiate confidence and competence, and if all else fails, manipulating the perceptions of others when necessary is a skill worth developing. Tear down that which rules you and use its ruin as fuel for the fire of your Will.

Summary

Sorcery is a tool through which intent is focused in order to manifest results. It is not dependent on any particular set of beliefs or techniques. Although physical objects and symbols are useful in assisting a sorcerer with this task, they are not essential.

Energy, in the literal sense of the capability to perform work, is one way of representing focused intent. By using laws of physics and thermodynamics as analogies for understanding how energy can be lost during its use, such loss can be counteracted or at least minimized. Barriers such as the inertia of external consensus reality, as well as the internal psychic censor must be overcome in order to exert Will effectively.

There are a number of methods through which the psychic censor can be temporarily circumvented. But I propose that exerting control over it and conditioning it to be more permissive, while still acting as an adequate filter to prevent the sorcerer from being overwhelmed by stimulus is more effective. You can accomplish this reprogramming in a number of ways, including pseudo-memetic self-conditioning and self-metaprogramming through the use of psychotropic substances. In addition to these possibilities, quantum sorcery exploits the rigid system of scientific education, and the implanted predisposition toward accepting and internalizing concepts which are presented under the auspices of science to introduce ideas which the censor might otherwise reject.

Although there is an inherent level of egotism necessary for working sorcery, there is also a need to interact successfully with the mundane world. A cultivated awareness of just how far from the norm will be tolerated by society before labeling an individual as dangerous to its structure can be a great benefit.

So far, I've introduced some of the principles of sorcery and presented a few practical concepts which can serve as a framework for what is to come. Now it's time to consider the physical forces and reality models that Quantum Sorcery draws upon.

Models of Physical Reality
The Macrocosm

Chapter 3
Quantum Reality

Those who are not shocked when they first come across
quantum mechanics cannot possibly have understood it.

– Niels Bohr

In chapter one, I investigated the belief that the act of divining the future through oracular methods has the effect of influencing the future. This implies that events which are observed can be changed by the very act of observation. In 1927, a new theory of how the mechanics of reality operate emerged that implied that this belief might be true. In this chapter, I present a very brief introduction to some of the concepts and theories of quantum mechanics in order to provide a foundation for understanding concepts which will be introduced throughout the rest of this book. I strongly encourage further investigation of these topics. A greater understanding of how matter and energy interact and relate at the most fundamental level becomes an invaluable asset to a sorcerer, whether in this system or any other.

Quantum mechanics as a discipline owes its development to a procession of distinguished physicists and mathematicians. Many of them were rivals who were actively supporting different models of the emerging discipline. In a number of cases, important discoveries were made by individuals or groups who were seeking to disprove opposing theories. In some cases, these were friendly rivalries, while in others there was a great deal of rancour.

Dave Smith

Quantum mechanics can trace its beginnings to the study of radiation. In 1859, Gustav Kirchhoff proposed a theory on thermal radiation which he later termed *blackbody* radiation. A blackbody is an object that perfectly absorbs and emits all energy which strikes it, and Kirchhoff concluded that the amount of energy emitted was based on the temperature and frequency of the energy. The theorem was released with a missing function which described precisely how these values related to total energy, and Kirchhoff challenged other physicists to find it. A number of partial solutions were suggested over the next 40 years, but none satisfied the relationship for all wavelengths of energy. It was not until 1900 that the solution was finally discovered by Max Planck (O'Connor and Robertson, 1996).

In order to write his formula, Planck assumed that atoms can absorb or emit energy only in discrete packets, which he referred to as *quanta*. This theory refuted ideas in classical physics, such as the view that energy flowed like liquid in a continuous stream. It was not until 1905 that it gained wider acceptance after being cited by Albert Einstein to explain the photoelectric effect. Planck resolved that there is a constant of proportionality between the frequency of a wave and its minimum energy. This is known as *Planck's constant*, and has a value of 1.05×10^{-27} gram-cm per second.

During this timeframe, the understanding of the structure of the atom itself was also revolutionized. The simple model put forth by Ernest Rutherford and refined by Niels Bohr, in which electrons orbited around a nucleus like planets around a star, was shown to be inadequate. One discovery was that the electrons were found to exert interference upon one another, behaving as if they were waves rather than particles. In addition, it was found that rather than following a stable and predictable orbit around the nucleus, the locations of the individual electrons could only be accurately represented as probability fields, where each was most likely to be found at any given time of observation. Further, the electrons seemed not to follow a predictable path as they, in effect, jumped from one probability field to another.

One of the physical properties of seemly solid matter that was revealed through experimentation is that it has a dual nature. Depending on the circumstances under which it is observed, matter appears to behave either as a particle or as a wave. If a single electron is projected toward a surface with two parallel slits cut in it and a solid surface behind the slits, then interference patterns can be observed as if that electron were a wave. If one of the slits is covered, and the experiment is repeated, then the interference pattern disappears. This implies that each electron is passing through both slits simultaneously and interfering with itself (Hawking, 1988). Yet that same electron can also be observed as a particle with properties such as mass and momentum which can be measured. When an electron is observed in this manner, the field of probabilities of its wave form is said to have *collapsed* into a single location in space. Until then, its exact state cannot be predicted.

Werner Heisenberg addressed this phenomenon in a paper published in 1927. He stated that the more precisely the position of a particle is determined, the less precisely its momentum is known. In other words, if the position of an electron is observed, then its wave properties lose relevance, and if the momentum of its wave form is observed, then its location as a particle in space becomes more difficult to predict. This became known as the *Uncertainty Principle*.

The new model that emerged in 1927 was known as the *Copenhagen Interpretation* of quantum mechanics. This was due to the work that Bohr, Heisenberg, and others had performed at Bohr's institute in Copenhagen, Denmark. This model incorporated particle/wave duality and observational influence on quantum states and was both championed and condemned by some of the most prominent physicists and mathematicians of the time. While defending the model, even Heisenberg admitted that "the measuring device has been constructed by the observer, and we have to remember that what we observe is not nature in itself, but nature exposed to our method of questioning" (Heisenberg, in Ferris 1991). Within existing mathematical and observational limitations, the models of quantum mechanics did well at explaining how matter and energy interact at an atomic level, but the theory was still considered to be lacking by many classical physicists.

Erwin Schrödinger considered quantum mechanics to be incomplete in its ability to describe the behaviour of matter at a larger scale. He illustrated this with his famous thought experiment in 1935 in which a cat is placed in a box with a radiation source and a cyanide gas capsule. If the radiation source emits a particle within a given time period, then the gas capsule will be ruptured, killing the cat. Until the box is opened, and the state of the system is observed, there is an equal chance that the particle has been emitted, and thus that the cat is either alive or dead. Under quantum mechanics, the probability is not collapsed into the actual state until the box is opened, thus it is the act of observation itself that is considered to be responsible for this collapse. Einstein also strongly resisted this theory, and in fact mocked it. He asked whether or not the universe changed every time a mouse looked at it.

The implication that an observer could have a measurable

effect on the behaviour of matter at the subatomic level was contrary to the model of the universe that most scientists had been operating under since the beginning of the nineteenth century. This model, put forth by the Marquis de Laplace, argued that the universe was completely deterministic. This meant that if the state of the universe could be determined at any point in time, then a set of laws should exist which would allow the calculation of any prior or future state. If quantum mechanics holds true, then this model is refuted; the universe is non-deterministic, and the ability to predict past and future states based on the present is eliminated.

Fundamental Particles and Forces

At several points in time, physicists have believed that they have identified the most fundamental particles of matter, but in each case later analysis has yielded another even smaller set of particles which combine to comprise those prior fundamental components. At first, the atom was thought to be the smallest unit of matter. This belief had held since its inception by the classical Greek philosopher Democritus who named this fundamental unit *atomos*, or indivisible. The atom was resolved into the nucleus and a swarm of electrons (which are just one of six varieties of a family of related particles known as *leptons*) by Ernest Rutherford in 1911. Next, in 1932, the nucleus was found by James Chadwick to be comprised of protons and neutrons. In 1964, Murray Gell-Mann mathematically derived the theory that protons and neutrons are each constructed out of three *quarks,* and so the idea of what exactly constitutes a fundamental particle was reduced in scale once more. Other quarks have been subsequently identified, and research at CERN in Switzerland, the Stanford Linear Accelerator Centre (SLAC) in California, and Fermilab in Illinois have revealed still more particles which result from the decay and collision of larger particles at high energy levels. As even more powerful particle accelerators, such as CERN's Large Hadron Collider have come online, it has become possible to discern particles at increasingly high energy levels.

Not all the particles that have been theorized can be detected. Some, such as *gravitons* and *gluons*, are virtual, and are used to better conceptualize force interactions between other particles. Collectively, these force carrying particles are referred to as *bosons* in honour of Indian physicist Satyendra Bose. Perhaps the most widely known among these is the Higgs boson, discovered in 2012 at CERN, and named in honour of Peter Higgs. He was one of a group of researchers who predicted its existence. This particle is thought to be responsible for conveying the property of mass to all other bosons.

One of the intrinsic properties attributed to fundamental particles is *spin*. It is considered to be analogous to angular velocity, as if the particle were rotating around an axis. This property was conceived in 1925 by George Uhlenbeck and Samuel Goudsmit to resolve the observation that electrons exhibited magnetic properties. All matter particles, like the electron itself, have been found to have a spin of one-half. These particles are collectively known as *fermions* in honour of Italian-American physicist Enrico Fermi. Most of the force-carrying bosons have been found to have a spin of one, except for the *graviton*, which has a spin of two. A group of theorized bosons which have not been experimentally verified are thought to have a spin of zero, or of fractions other than one-half.

Based upon the exchange of the force-carrying bosons between particles, four fundamental forces have been identified which describe the way in which matter interacts. These are gravitation, electromagnetism, the strong nuclear force, and the weak nuclear force. It is possible that there are other forces, as of yet undiscovered and unobserved, but these four are capable of explaining the behaviour of matter in the current state of the universe. In a very young universe, infinitesimal fractions of a second after the "Big Bang", it is thought at that all four forces become one, so it is theoretically feasible to suggest that as the universe continues to cool and expand, that other forces might yet emerge.

Gravitational force operates between all particles with mass, attracting equally regardless of charge or state. It is capable of acting over long distances. This boson for this force, the *graviton*, is a massless particle which travels at the speed of light. At a quantum level, this force has been found to be far weaker than the other three. The M-theory model of matter, which is discussed in greater detail later in this chapter, has suggested that this weakness is due to the loss of much of the graviton's energy into extra-dimensional space.

The *electromagnetic force* affects only charged particles such as electrons and has no effect upon particles which have no charge. This force also has a polarity, either negative or positive. Charges with opposite polarities are attracted to one another, while identical charges repel. This force is far stronger than gravity and holds electrons in orbit around the positively charged protons in the atomic nucleus. The boson of electromagnetism, the *photon*, is massless, and represents the minimum possible energy quanta of this force.

The *weak nuclear force* affects the particles which comprise matter, such as electrons, protons, and neutrons. Its force is limited to distances smaller than an atomic nucleus. This force is also responsible for the property of radioactivity. This force is carried by two particles, the *W* and *Z bosons*. These are comparatively large, yet short-lived compared to the other force-carrying particles.

The *strong nuclear force* binds quarks together to form protons and neutrons, as well as holding these resultant particles together in the atomic nucleus. This is the strongest of the fundamental forces, and its boson is known as the *gluon*.

Each type of particle also has an associated *antiparticle*, which has the same mass, but opposite charge, spin, and nuclear force. Paul Dirac proposed the first antiparticle, the *positron*, as part of a 1928 paper explaining the spin of electrons. This particle was subsequently observed experimentally by Carl Anderson in 1932. If a particle and its antiparticle come in contact with one another, they annihilate one another, releasing secondary particles and a large quantity of energy. One question that has persisted through the ongoing study of fundamental particles is why all the matter in the early universe was not annihilated by collisions of the ostensibly balanced quantity of particles and antiparticles. In other words, why is there *something* rather than *nothing*? In 2020, a Japanese project designed to study *neutrinos*, fast-moving, nearly massless particles which are released by the nuclear reactions in stars, determined that there is apparently an imbalance in the quantity of matter, in the form of neutrinos, over anti-matter in the form of antineutrinos. This may be indicative of imbalances in the decay of heavier particles in the early universe (Abe et al, 2020).

Collectively all these particles and the non-gravitational forces have been incorporated into what is known as the *Standard Model* of particle physics. However, this model is still incomplete. To reconcile the included particles and forces, there are 19 parameters which must be defined and entered into the quantum equations to cause the equations to match experimentally derived results. The model also fails to include gravitational force. Bringing this last force into the model and essentially *quantizing* general relativity has become what some physicists have referred to as "the Holy Grail of physics."

Unification

At the smallest theorized levels of reality, all dimensionality and time break down into what has been called *quantum foam* (Greene, 1999). The scale at which this effect is thought to be visible is below approximately 10^{-35} meters long, a distance known as the *Planck length*. Below this ultramicroscopic level, quantum fluctuations disrupt electromagnetic and gravitational fields which look stable at a larger scale. It is at this level where the smooth space-time model of general relativity breaks down. From a desire to reconcile the differing models, physicists began looking at new ways to mathematically relate the two competing theories, just as they have with the fundamental forces.

In 1967, several researchers working independently proposed theories which combined the weak nuclear force with the electromagnetic force. Following this advancement were attempts to combine these forces with the strong nuclear force to create a grand unified theory, or GUT. As Stephen Hawking observed: "This title is rather an exaggeration: the resultant theories are not all that grand, nor are they fully unified, as they do not include gravity" (Hawking, 1988). In addition, the energy level required to reconcile these three forces as one is approximately 10^{-13} times greater than the capacity of existing particle accelerators, so any theoretical solution is currently impossible to verify experimentally. Attempting to combine gravity into the GUT has yielded several theories, including *supergravity* and *string theory.*

The theory of supergravity combines another theory, known as *supersymmetry* with traditional general relativity. In the supersymmetry model, each fundamental matter particle, or fermion is thought to have a force-carrying boson counterpart known as a *superpartner.* In the specific case of supergravity, the force-carrying graviton is thought to have a counterpart, the *gravitino* which is as of yet too small to be detected. Supergravity theory also embraces the concept first proposed by Theodore Kaluza in 1919 that there are additional, imperceptible dimensions "curled up" inside of infinitesimal space. In 1995, Edward Witten theorized that supergravity was a specific case of one of the models of string theory.

String theory represents the smallest components of matter as one-dimensional vibrating filaments rather than as point particles. They are theorized to be approximately 10^{-35} meters in size. Strings are thought to appear as point particles only due to the limitations of instruments to distinguish dimensionality at such an ultramicroscopic scale. This visualisation places more emphasis on the wavelike nature of matter than preceding theories do. Different vibrational frequencies of individual strings are thought to account for the differences in, and presence of, the various fundamental particles. Five different models of this theory emerged, each of which satisfied the parameters of the overall model. It was thought at first that one was correct, and four would eventually be ruled out experimentally, but research has shown that all five seem to be different ways of describing the same overarching theory (Greene, 1999).

In 1995 Edward Witten created the M-theory in an attempt to reconcile the five individual string theories with supergravity. According to Witten, "M stands for magic, mystery or matrix, according to taste." This combined theory assumes the existence of 11 dimensions, ten of space and one of time, and also assumes that strings are the fundamental building blocks of matter. Besides strings, two dimensional *membranes*, and higher-dimensional structures known generically as p-branes are also part of the theory. A brane structure which contains a massive amount of energy could grow large enough to contain the entire known universe. This massive brane would have to exist as a feature in a larger, higher dimensional space.

Disagreement remains among physicists as to which of the various reality models is most likely to answer the greatest number of questions, as well as explain disputed but experimentally observed interactions among particles which contradict widely accepted theories in classical views of physics.

Quantum Entanglement

One of these ways in which quantum systems apparently violate prior models is known as *quantum entanglement*. This state occurs in certain scenarios in which the observable properties of one particle are inextricably tied to the properties of another. This effect is also referred to as *non-locality*, as it violates the principle of *locality* which states that events occurring at one point in space should have no immediate effect on those at another location. This is a consequence of the theory of special relativity, which states that information cannot travel faster than the speed of light.

One implication of non-locality is that quantum states can be measured or altered without direct observation. If two particles become entangled, then the state of one of these can be determined or altered in a known way by observing or manipulating its counterpart. Einstein felt that the possibility of this phenomenon suggested by quantum mechanics indicated that the theory must be incomplete and must contain hidden variables. If this were true then the theory was not an accurate description of reality, it was merely a statistical approximation.

In a debate with Bohr, Einstein referred to this proposed violation of locality as "spooky action at a distance." He published a thought exercise with Boris Podolsky and Nathan Rosen in 1935 to refute the completeness of quantum mechanics, which has come to be known as the EPR paradox. In 1964, John Bell disputed the incorporation of hidden variables. He published a set of mathematical relations, now known as Bell's inequalities, to support his position and illustrate the validity of non-local effects in a pair of entangled particles.

In 1982, a research team led by Alain Aspect experimentally verified that two photons emitted from the same atom in opposite directions were capable of affecting each other's behaviour at a distance without exchanging any detectable signal through space. As Aspect (1999) states in a later article:

> *We must conclude that an entangled EPR photon pair is a non-separable object; that is, it is impossible to assign individual local properties (local physical reality) to each photon. In some sense, both photons keep in contact through space and time.*

In 1998, another research group led by Gregor Weihs confirmed the findings of Aspect's team in an experiment which increased the distance between the observation points of the entangled particles from 12 meter distance used in the prior study to 400 meters in order to more rigorously enforce the conditions of the original EPR scenario (Weihs et al, 1998).

Although it was previously assumed that deep cooling and spatial distance were necessary to protect the entangled state of a system, In 2020, Jia Kong and colleagues have obtained results that imply otherwise. They were able to create a massive field of entangled gaseous Rubidium atoms at 450 Kelvin. Too, they showed that when an entangled system was perturbed by a random interaction, the entangled state information was not destroyed, but rather passed on to the intruding atom (Kong et al, 2020).

Summary

The study of radiation led Planck to discover that atoms can absorb or emit energy only in discrete packets, which he named quanta. At the same time, the structure of the atom itself was found to be far more complex than was originally thought. The movement of electrons as they orbit the nucleus was found to be better expressed as regions of probability rather than as rigid paths. In addition, the electrons were found to exhibit interference upon one another as they orbited, as if they were waves rather than particles. The dual nature of matter was further verified by the twin slit experiment which alternately caused electrons to manifest in these two ways.

In trying to define the behaviour of the newly discovered Werner Heisenberg formulated his Uncertainty Principle in 1927 which stated that fundamental properties of a subatomic particle, such as its exact position and momentum cannot both be known simultaneously, as the act of measuring one of these properties diminishes the relevance of the other.

In 1927 Heisenberg collaborated with Niels Bohr and other physicists in Denmark to produce what is known as the Copenhagen Interpretation of quantum mechanics. It did well at explaining how matter and energy interact at an atomic level, but was criticized by other physicists, including Albert Einstein and Erwin Schrödinger who created his "cat in a box" thought experiment to illustrate its limitations.

As a greater understanding of fundamental particles emerged, so did the definition of the fundamental forces of gravity, electromagnetism, and the strong and weak nuclear forces which act on them. The latter three forces were incorporated into the Standard Model of particle physics, but gravity remained un-reconciled with the others. The desire to describe the relationships between the three standard forces led to the Grand Unified Theory, or GUT, which cannot currently be verified experimentally.

Mathematical attempts at incorporating gravity into the GUT led to the creation of the supergravity and string theories, the latter of which proposed that matter was composed of Planck distance-sized one-dimensional vibrating filaments. Five different versions of string theory were eventually developed. Ultimately, M-theory emerged to unify all of these as well as supergravity.

Even as the current theories have provided explanations for much of the observed behaviour of matter and energy, there are still numerous unanswered questions and unexplained properties of particle interaction. The state of quantum entanglement, originally cited by Einstein to illustrate the incompleteness of quantum mechanics was analysed mathematically by John Bell, who created a set of functions which seem to validate non-local effects in a pair of entangled particles. Alain Aspect and other researchers have carried out a series of experiments which have demonstrated the capability for non-local information awareness between entangled particles, apparently violating Einstein's special theory of relativity.

An understanding of physics provides a sorcerer with a potent set of tools for visualisation, as well as a set of symbols which can be used for manipulating reality. At the ultramicroscopic scale, the fabric of space and time are theorized to be a chaotic storm of quantum foam where violent fluctuations disrupt electromagnetic and gravitational fields. At this level of abstraction, possibility and probability are functionally interchangeable and hidden dimensions lie curled in on themselves at all points in known space. This is matter and energy at its most primal form, where Will can be exerted to supplant chance.

Chapter 4
The Implicate Order

In a holographic universe there are no limits to the extent to which we can alter the fabric of reality.

– Michael Talbot

The process of trying to understand the implications of quantum mechanics has generated several offshoot theories among the physicists and mathematicians who have studied it. Some of these ideas have withered under the scrutiny of the peer review process, and others which could not be experimentally proven have been relegated to the realm of metaphysics. One theory that has managed to continue to straddle the boundary between hard science and philosophy is the *implicate order* theory proposed by David Bohm. Opponents have acknowledged its elegance, as well as their respect for its creator, even as they have felt obligated to repudiate the theory itself. This theory, if it is ultimately found to be valid, has implications that consciousness and reality are inextricably bound together.

The experimental verification of the phenomenon of non-local interaction between entangled particles seems to indicate that the scenario described in the EPR paradox does in fact occur. This finding vindicated the position of Bohm, who had worked a great deal on the theoretical framework of this problem. While writing a textbook on the Copenhagen interpretation of quantum mechanics in 1951, Bohm had begun to question the non-deterministic nature of quantum interactions. He believed that there must be an underlying structure which was responsible for the apparently random behaviour of matter and energy at the smallest scale.

Bohm sent a copy of his book to Albert Einstein, who praised him for his clear presentation of the subject matter. This led to a series of conversations between the two about the limitations of quantum mechanics and the fundamental conflicts between this model and Einstein's own theory of relativity. The following year, Bohm produced two papers in which he began to define his own model, which came to be known as the *causal interpretation* of quantum mechanics.

The causal interpretation states that the movement and behaviour of subatomic particles is not random but is determined by a force which he referred to as *quantum potential*. Bohm proposed that this force directs the movement of particles by providing them with active information about their environment similar to the way that reflected radar signals inform a ship of its surroundings.

In 1959, Bohm and his student Yakir Aharonov discovered that in some cases electrons were able to detect the presence of a magnetic field even if that field was shielded from them. This became known as the Aharonov-Bohm effect, and Bohm believed that it affirmed his theory that there must be some type of unseen connection between quantum systems other than the known fundamental forces (Pratt, 1993).

By the 1960s, Bohm had begun to formulate his own theory as to what kind of underlying structure could be responsible for the non-deterministic behaviour of particles and would also explain his findings in his work with quantum potential. The conclusion he arrived at was that the fragmented view of matter that had resulted from an acceptance of quantum mechanics was an illusion, and that all physical reality is in fact an undivided whole which he referred to as the *implicate order*. This term, from the Latin *plicare*, which means "to fold", indicates that the true nature which cannot be directly perceived is folded in on itself. This is distinguished from the *explicate* or "unfolded" order which is the phenomenal universe which can be perceived. In this model of reality, all particle behaviour exhibited by matter is simply an observational abstraction of the real movement of the underlying whole.

To demonstrate the way in which the implicate order is folded, Bohm referred to an experiment which he had seen on television. This consisted of a pair of glass cylinders nested concentrically with a thin space between them. This space was filled with a viscous, clear liquid. The top of the apparatus had a mechanism by which the outer cylinder could be made to turn, while the liquid and inner cylinder remained static. A drop of ink was injected into the liquid, and the cylinder was turned. As the outer cylinder turned, the drop of ink was extruded into a thin coloured thread. If this process was continued, eventually the ink completely disappeared from view. It had in effect been enfolded into the liquid. When the outer cylinder was turned in reverse, the ink thread reappeared out of the clear liquid, and eventually, the thread reverted to the original ink drop. This display made Bohm realise that when the ink was diffused through the clear liquid, it was not in a state of disorder, as it seemed, but in fact exhibited a hidden order.

Having reached the conclusion that the implicate order was the missing piece in his own causal interpretation of quantum mechanics, Bohm also postulated that the implicate order is not the ultimate reality but is itself only a projection of a *superimplicate* order. He proposed that there could be an infinite number of orders, possibly of a hierarchical nature, each of which is influenced and defined by the order above it in the series (Pratt).

Matter as a Hologram

As an analogy for describing the appearance of individual units of matter as part of the undivided whole, Bohm suggested that the implicate order be compared to a hologram. A hologram is a type of image created through the use of a laser. The laser light is passed through a half-silvered mirror which splits it into two beams. The first split portion of the beam passes through the mirror and continues directly onto a photographic plate. The other portion of the original beam reflects off of the mirror and onto an object. Its light is scattered off of the object and then onto the plate as well. As the two portions of the split beam re-converge on the plate, an interference pattern is created and is recorded.

When the interference pattern recorded on the plate is illuminated with laser light again, the object appears not as a flat photographic image, but rather as a three-dimensional structure. More remarkably, if the image plate is shattered, and one of the shards is illuminated, the entire object can still be viewed, although with a lesser degree of detail and with a decreased range of possible view angles than the original had. There is no direct correlation between parts of the originally recorded object and parts of its image on the plate; rather every divisible portion of the image contains the whole. The image of the whole is contained in each region of space. This inspired Bohm (1980) to state that:

> There is the germ of a new notion of order here. This order is not to be understood solely in terms of a regular arrangement of objects (e.g., in rows) or as a regular arrangement of events (e.g. in a series). Rather a total order is contained, in some implicit sense, in each region of space and time.

By way of further example, visual images can be translated into a sequence of signals which can be carried on radio waves. The position of a given point in the transmitted wave form does not necessarily have any direct correlation to any given point in the original image. The waves carry the image in an implicate order. When received, the image is then explicated from the waves and displayed.

Radio and light waves are not unique in their ability to carry enfolded order. Electron beams, sound waves, or any other type of wave propagation are also capable of the same action, which at its most fundamental level is simply the transmission of information. Bohm called this collective concept the *holomovement*.

The Holomovement

The holomovement is the carrier wave by which the implicate order is transmitted. It is in a constant state of flux and is undefinable and immeasurable. All theories in physics can be considered to abstract only a certain aspect of it that is relevant within in a limited context of study. This explains the fact that although the theories contradict one another in a number of ways, that both quantum mechanics and general relativity can be said to be correct within their own frame of reference. The attempt to tie these theories together only fails due to the disparities in scope which each one pertains to.

Within this paradigm, structures may be folded into the implicate order to differing degrees, and as they unfold, they become manifest as quantifiable points. This creates the perception of a "whole system of objects in continuous movement and interaction (Bohm)." The degree to which a structure is enfolded dictates a dimensional value, which Bohm considered to be analogous to time, which describes the degree or amount of explication which would need to occur in order to reveal the structure. This process is manifest in quantum mechanics as a particle abstracted from the greater whole. The track followed by the particle as it is observed is merely a local aspect which has meaning only within the immediate frame of reference. Within this reference, it is the rapid sequential unfolding of a series of similar forms which generates the illusion of persistence. This effect can be most easily visualised as the illusion of movement created by flip-book animation or motion picture film.

This idea can be addressed in the terminology of sorcery by returning to the principle of the manipulation of symbols. The particle, along with its associated energy, mass, movement, charge etc. can be interpreted as a symbol for the implicate process which underlies it. By using this abstracted interface, the conscious mind can be provided with the tools of organization and hierarchy which satisfy its needs to deal in tangible concepts, even as the subconscious mind is allowed to interact with the intangible field of potential which the interface obscures. A model which attempts to describe this interaction between mind and the holomovement will be discussed in greater detail in a later chapter.

Quantum Effects in the Implicate Order

The theory of implicate order provides explanations behind several concepts of quantum mechanics that otherwise seem non-intuitive. The most immediate of these is the non-locality of the EPR paradox. Even though this principle has been validated experimentally, some physicists still resist or ignore the findings, as the results deviate too far from the widely accepted Standard Model. Bohm described a simple scenario which illustrates what he considered the error in perception which has become encoded into the dogma of particle physics.

In this analogy, two video cameras are aimed at a fish in a hidden aquarium from different angles. An observer is shown only the monitors which display each image. By watching the images, a relationship between the behaviours of what appears to be two different fish can be observed. When one fish moves, the other fish is seen to move as well. The two never seem to be identically oriented, but their movement will always seem to be related. When two entangled particles exhibit a non-local effect on one another, the relationship between them is similar to the two views of the same fish. In terms of observational reality, it is intuitive to treat the two particles as separate, but if viewed in the framework of the implicate order; they can be described as two three-dimensional projections of the same object contained in a higher-dimensional reality (Bohm).

Not just particle interactions, but the dual particle / wave nature of matter itself can also be viewed as an artifact of perception when viewed in the framework of the implicate order. Yet another analogy is suggested to illustrate this principle. Consider a stream of turbulent flowing water as a representation of the holomovement in its state of constant flux. As transient features such as vortices and eddies manifest in the stream, they have coherent identities as structures in their own right, with local sets of conditions which govern their behaviour, as well as spatial boundaries inside of which this behaviour is dominant over the base conditions of the larger stream. Even so, these structures are still part of the larger stream as a whole, and when conditions have changed in such a way that these features are no longer viable, the material which comprised them is once again indistinguishable from the rest. When interference patterns manifest as standing waves in the holomovement, an observable, yet transient structure is also created for as long as conditions are favourable. This pattern becomes temporarily explicated as a point particle. Just as in the case of the vortices and eddies, this structure too will be reabsorbed by the material from which it was formed.

Fragmentation

David Bohm did not develop his theories from a purely mechanistic standpoint; he also reflected a great deal of his philosophy into them as well. He believed that the perception of fragmentation in quantum mechanics was only part of a greater, and to him more distressing trend penetrating society as well as each individual. This is evidenced in society through the separation of mankind into different nations, religions, and political groups, and individually through the compartmentalization of the human psyche into competing loyalties, desires, and ambitions. Bohm felt that all of these divisions were illusionary and detrimental.

Bohm was an admirer of Indian philosopher and former Theosophist Jiddo Krishnamurti. The two corresponded regularly, and Bohm found a parallel between Krishnamurti's teachings and his own theories. Both were convinced that the limitations on human faculties of perception, thought, and memory were responsible for fragmentation and conflict in the world. This association was criticized by some of Bohm's contemporaries who worried that he was drifting too far afield from physics and into the metaphysical realm. A similar affinity for mentalist Uri Gellar led a colleague to warn Bohm that their work could be jeopardized by a perceived endorsement of Geller and his claims of psychokinetic ability (Gardner, 2000).

Dave Smith

Although Bohm's drift through his career toward the spiritual frustrated many of his supporters, most have continued to acknowledge his contributions as a theoretical physicist. Physicist Jack Sarfatti has commented that "There are two Bohm's. Bohm, The Physicist and Bohm the New Age Mystic. Do not confound the two (Mutnick)."

Summary

David Bohm experienced a paradigm shift in his beliefs about the nature of matter and existence as a whole as a result of his attempts to find hidden variables within quantum mechanics. He developed his own causal interpretation of the theory which stated that in addition to the known fundamental forces, an undetected guiding force known as quantum potential acted on particle systems.

As he further developed his ideas on the structure of matter, Bohm created the concept of the implicate order, a level of enfolded reality which is merely abstracted in the explicate or unfolded order which can be perceived. This implicate order is based on the movement and flux of information through electromagnetic and other waveforms in a process called the holomovement.

Like a hologram, each portion of the implicate order which can be abstracted and observed can be considered to contain the entirety of the whole which it represents. Bohm believed that observational limitations and misunderstandings, coupled with a human propensity to embrace fragmentation are responsible for the structures interpreted by physicists as particles within the field of quantum mechanics.

To apply this model of reality in a framework of sorcery, these abstracted particles can be viewed as symbols which can be used to manipulate the underlying implicate order. Each fragmentary portion of reality which can be influenced will result in a corresponding influence over a larger whole. This model is subtle and very deep, requiring a well-developed capability for visualisation to effectively use it. As I will discuss later in a later chapter, this theory has profound implications when considered in tandem with the holonomic mind model proposed by Karl Pribram.

Chapter 5
The Fractal Multiverse

The structure of the multiverse is determined by information flow.

– David Deutsch

The idea of parallel universes is probably familiar to anyone who reads works of Science Fiction or Fantasy. The concept in general is that there are other realities which contain similar but different, versions of our own world. In certain situations, the protagonist somehow crosses into such a universe, or has interactions with someone who has crossed into his. What fewer people are probably aware of is the fact that a number of theories in physics suggest that parallel universes are not fiction, but actually exist. One of these suggests that when one possible outcome in an experiment actually occurs, all possibilities have occurred, but only one of them happened in the universe which the observer inhabits. This creates an opportunity for the application of sorcery through the possibility that the Will can have an effect on directing the observer into the universe in which a specific desired outcome is the one which happened.

In this chapter I will introduce several of the theories for describing parallel universes that have been suggested, and how each type is thought to solve various problems which have been identified in quantum mechanics. Some of the theories are not as applicable as others to the scenario described above, but an awareness of their processes can still be valuable as a tool for modelling magical endeavours, so I have included material on those as well.

Many Worlds

The paradox created by the double-slit experiment described in chapter three has led to a number of explanations as to what exactly happens when a single quanta of energy seems to going through both slits simultaneously. For example, the Copenhagen interpretation postulates that a quantum system can be characterized by a *state vector*. This state vector, also known as a wave function, can be thought of as a mathematical expression of the possible attributes of system. When the system is observed, the vector collapses, and the various possible states of the system are resolved into a single state. This explanation was deemed unsatisfactory by some physicists who began to search for alternate theories which could provide a different answer to what had come to be known as the *measurement problem*. The problem was that even though each quantum system could be modelled mathematically to be in different simultaneous states, whenever such a system was measured, it was found to be in a single state (of location, momentum, etc.)

In 1957, Princeton physicist Hugh Everett proposed a new theory, which he referred to as the *relative state* interpretation (Barrett, 2003). This theory held that any measurement of a quantum system would create a complex system in which the state of the system being measured could only be defined relative to the one measuring it. Mechanically speaking, each time a quantum experiment such as the double-slit is performed, all outcomes actually occur. The results which were not manifest in the observer's world (Everett's term for what is typically referred to as universe) occurred in other worlds which are considered to have split from the observer's world at the moment that the state of the system was observed. Rather than having individual state vectors for each separate event, in the relative state model the entirety of any given world can be represented by a single state vector, which does not collapse.

Put in terms of Schrödinger's work, when a number of choices are possible, and the outcome is not yet known, a quantum system (or cat) is said to be in a state of *superposition*. This is a fragile state of existence which is broken by interaction with another quantum system, such as a researcher looking into a box to see if the cat is alive or dead. The process by which a single state is manifest into an objective universe, to the exclusion of all other possible states, is known as *decoherence*. This is the process which keeps observers in one world from perceiving the split which creates parallel counterparts. One way of envisioning this effect in action is by the analogy of a pencil perfectly balanced on its tip. This constitutes its superposition. When interacted with, by a photon of light striking it for example, the pencil can fall in any direction. The direction which any particular observer sees the pencil fall in their frame of reference is due to decoherence.

Although considered to be a mathematically sound and valid theory by those who reviewed it, Everett's work received little attention from the quantum physics community. In 1970 Bryce DeWitt, who had been one of Everett's reviewers, began a campaign to re-popularize Everett's theory. In this process, he gave it the name it is better known by, the *many worlds* interpretation. DeWitt had previously worked with Princeton physicist John Wheeler (who had been Everett's dissertation advisor) in 1965 to create the Wheeler-DeWitt equation, which attempts to combine general relativity with quantum mechanics. With DeWitt's assistance, Everett's paper was included in a book along with articles by other prominent physicists, and his theory began to receive a greater degree of exposure.

Although this interpretation is still subject to a great deal of scepticism, polls of physicists have indicated that only the Copenhagen interpretation itself has more adherents when it comes to explaining the measurement problem. A number of younger physicists have taken up Everett and DeWitt's position, and have begun a new effort to prove its validity.

The Hierarchy of Plausibility

One of the leaders in the effort to further define how the many worlds theory operates in physical reality is MIT physicist Max Tegmark. Tegmark has explored some of the possible scenarios which describe how parallel universes relate to one another with regard to the familiar dimensionalities of space and time. In his summary he identifies four levels of structure, based on theoretical levels of plausibility to explain the various possibilities.

Level 1 parallel universes are those which are theorized to exist adjacent to one another in space. If this is so, then the neighbour to our own universe must lay beyond the maximum visible extent of ours. This distance is estimated to be approximately 4×10^{26} meters (Tegmark, 2004). A sphere having this radius is known as the *Hubble volume*, and is functionally equivalent to "our" universe. Tegmark asserts that the Level 1 model is the most widely accepted among those who subscribe to the many worlds interpretation, although each model has its proponents. A second type, or Level 2 "inflationary" model exists. I will not go into details about it here, as I cover them in greater detail later in this chapter.

Everett's theory predicts universes which are classified as

Level 3 in Tegmark's system. Unlike the Level 1 model, rather than existing remotely in space, Level 3 parallel universes exist in relatively close proximity to one another. Rather than being spatially separate, they exist in different states of *Hilbert Space*. The topic of this space itself is complex, but for the purpose of this text, it can be thought of as the "place" where the functions which completely describe the states of quantum systems "happen". Within this space, multiple universes could spatially overlap one another completely, but not be perceivable. The number of possible universes of this type is vast, but not infinite. Tegmark suggests a limit of $10,000,000,000^{115}$, but admits that this number is a conservative estimate (Tegmark).

Level 4 parallel universes are based on the premise that all universes are in fact mathematical structures, and that all sentient life forms are self-aware substructures within these constructs. Other instances of these speculative universes might have radically different mathematical systems, laws of physics, etc. This model is based on the speculations that our own world might be a mathematical structure, and that all mathematical structures are reflected in physical structures somewhere as well.

Each of the potential models in this system has arisen based on theories that have been proposed at various points in time, and each can be useful when visualised as a technique for directing the self into a particular universe where the reality desired is manifest.

The Multiverse of Information

Oxford University researcher David Deutsch is of the opinion that the term *multiverse* should be used to describe the collection of parallel universes. In his model, a universe is a global construct consisting of the whole of space and its contents at a given time. He supports Everett's model of many worlds in that he believes that parallel universes are defined by their location in Hilbert Space, as opposed to being spatially adjacent to one another. In this interpretation of the model, such universes cannot influence their counterparts via quantum interference. Each universe begins with a set of initial conditions which it inherits at the moment of its creation through decoherence. All subsequent development in that universe is based on its physical laws acting upon these initial conditions. No further possibilities for interaction with any other universes is possible; only subsequent splits into additional branches. This is a result of the assertion that decoherence is an irreversible process.

While this view is consistent with the concept of the Level 3 universe, another aspect of Deutsch's theory is closer to the Level 4 in Tegmark's hierarchy. Deutsch invokes the concept of "universality of computation" to assert that by studying quantum information networks, particularly quantum computing, that the behaviour of information flow for all quantum systems in general can be analysed (Deutsch, 2002). Through modelling the flow of *qubits*, or quantum bits through theoretical circuits and logic gates, Deutsch has also proposed that non-locality is a fallacy resulting from the fact that quantum systems can store information in a state which requires interaction with those systems (via decoherence) in order to access the information contained within them (Deutsch and Hayden, 1999). He does not dispute the existence of quantum entanglement, but within his model, it is considered a local effect involving the exchange of information between particles at sub-light speed.

One of the most important aspects of this model as it applies to sorcery is that it illustrates once more the axiom from the Emerald Tablet of Hermes Trismegistus: What is above is like what is below. What is below is like what is above. The microcosm of a quantum computer reflects the behaviour of all quantum effects in the multiverse. Deutsch does not imply such two-way causality in this equivalence, but this is the threshold where sorcery must take over from science, using scientific models and methods for its own purposes. Many ideas which have become accepted as reality within science began in the form of thought experiments conducted by adepts whose language of symbolic manipulation is mathematics. Through the use of these symbols, those who model the processes of the universe also mould the physical universe itself.

Level 2 Parallel Universes: The Inflationary Model

Not all models of parallel universe development are based on explaining the collapse, or lack thereof, of the state vector of a quantum system. Some are based in *cosmology*, the study of the structure and development of the universe. This discipline is carried out in part by observing the *cosmic background radiation*. This is microwave radiation which remains from the cooling of the initial hot state of the universe typically described in the Big Bang theory. Through studying the density, distribution, and waveforms of this radiation, information about the expansion, shape, and development of the universe can be learned.

In 1981, Stanford cosmologist Alan Guth announced his theory of *cosmic inflation* based on work that he began in 1979 in an attempt to reconcile the big bang theory of cosmology with the observed distribution of matter and energy in the observable universe. The inflationary theory states that the early universe went through a stage of exponential expansion as it cooled. Matter coalesced and interacted with energy fields which effectively caused a strong anti-gravitational effect to rapidly expand the universe. (Guth, 1997). This effect was very short-lived, lasting possibly 10-35 seconds.

This expansion provided possible answers for several problems which had been unreconciled in the big bang theory. One of these is the uniformity with which matter and energy are distributed throughout the universe. Observations of the cosmic background radiation have also shown that its temperature is incredibly uniform in all directions. Such uniformity is thought to have been achieved only 300,000 years after the big bang itself. For such a uniformity to occur, even at such an early stage of development in the universe, the heat would have had to dissipate at nearly 100 times the speed of light. Another problem solved by the expansion theory is the observed flatness of the universe. General relativity predicts that it should appear to be curved, but physical observation has shown it to be flat within the scale of the observable universe (Linde, 1994).

Although the causal force behind Guth's theory was found inaccurate, his basic premise was sound, and attracted the attention of a number of other physicists. In 1982, Russian physicist Andre Linde expounded on Guth's ideas, and by the following year he released his own theory which he called *chaotic inflation*. In this model, no anti-gravity or cooling are assumed to be responsible for expansion, rather the effect is assumed to be due to *scalar fields*. Scalar fields are multi-dimensional areas to which a single numeric value for a measurable property such as magnetic force or electrical charge is uniform throughout their space. In this case, these values would describe the energy levels present within the field. These fields, which develop through the actions of quantum fluctuations, affect particles with mass by making them heavier. Massless particles such as photons are not affected. Linde considered all possible scalar fields which were thought to be present in the early universe and checked to see if their values could have caused inflation by interacting with matter in the incipient universe.

What Linde determined was that the particles which were interacting with scalar fields lost energy at a far slower rate than particles which were not involved in such interactions. This resulted in regions in the young universe which by virtue of their higher energy levels sustained a higher rate of expansion as other regions around them lost their energy and slowed. As the fields which were influencing matter dissipated, these areas ceased their inflation and began to reach equilibrium. However, not all scalar fields dissipate. In some rare areas, the fields are enhanced by further quantum fluctuations which lead to a continuing exponential inflation. This effect is capable of continuing unabated and generating new volumes in space which constitute new universes, which then in turn do the same. Linde refers to this effect as *eternal inflation.*

There might be an infinite number of universes created in this manner, and they may have vastly different degrees of dimensionality and different laws of physics than ours. Because of this different dimensionality, they could spatially overlap our own universe, yet not be detectable to observers living in any of them.

The importance of the Level 2 parallel universe to sorcery lies more in its model than in its cosmological implications. The effect of cascading creation given a small initial impetus is the primary mechanism through which quantum sorcery is manifest. This effect taking place at the macro scale of the universe is directly analogous to the effect of starting a cascade of effects at the quantum micro scale. This latter application of the effect will be discussed in more detail later.

With specific regard to the mechanism by which these universes are created, the scalar field, there is another potential application to sorcery as well. Through the application of virtual scalar fields visualised and modelled by the sorcerer, intent can be amplified, even within the objective universe. The structures created by such an exercise of this visualised inflation will be *fractal*, even as the parallel universes created by the actual mechanism are.

Fractal Forms and Infinite Scale

Mathematician Benoit Mandelbrot investigated a seemingly simple problem in the 1970s: "How long is the coast of Britain?" What he found was that as the degree of scale employed in the measurement was taken to finer levels, the longer the coastline appeared to be. This was a result of smaller and smaller features appearing as the perspective was magnified. Features which appear to be straight lines on a small-scale map are revealed to be complicated and jagged on a large scale map. He referred to these forms as fractal, from the Latin for "broken". When fractal functions are graphed, the results can be viewed at any level of magnification, and they will appear similar.

According to Mandelbrot, the specific frame of reference for this was actually an academic Trojan horse designed to present his pre-existing ideas on fractal dimensionality to a previously unreceptive mathematics community (Mandelbrot, 1967). The Mandelbrot set, as it is now called, is an *iterative function* which describes points on a plane. This means that the function operates on results from previous runs, and that these results correspond to points on a two-dimensional surface. As this calculation is run through hundreds to thousands of iterations, and the results graphed, the result is a complex shape which possesses a degree of similarity on an infinite scale.

As previously mentioned, Linde's chaotic inflation model produces a fractal pattern of universes. This is only one instance in which the concept of fractal geometry which Mandelbrot championed can be found in nature. It is also found in hydrological systems, the circulatory system in the body, and in the vein patterns in leaves. In these cases, small systems of relative simplicity merge to create larger, complex systems.

The study of fractal geometry can be a useful tool for understanding the concept of the continuum of scale in magical workings. By exerting intent at the smallest possible scale, where reality is the most malleable, the greatest effect can be achieved for the amount of energy invested. In addition, the propagation of this minute influence into the universe at large through the assembly of simple threads altered by sorcery can be visualised as an iterative function. Consistent belief in the ability to exert influence at the micro scale will result in greater success in influencing the macro scale.

4-Brane Collisions

In chapter three I introduced M-theory, the attempt by Edward Witten to find a grand unified theory by combining the five string theories with supergravity. One of the features in this theory is the concept of the brane, a multi-dimensional structure of varying size and energy that exists in a larger spatial dimension. A one-brane, or one-dimensional brane is simply another term for a string. Branes are thought to have the capability of growing large enough to contain an entire universe on their multi-dimensional surface.

Within this model, one of the areas of interest is the interaction between adjacent four-dimensional branes in five-dimensional or *bulk* space. A team of physicists comprised of Justin Khoury, Burt A. Ovrut, Paul J. Steinhardt, and Neil Turok proposed that the big bang was caused by an impact between two such 4-branes. This model is known as the *Ekpyrotic universe*. This term is derived from the Greek *ekpyrosis*, which refers to a process by which the universe is cyclically consumed by, and reconstituted from, fire. It is part of the model of cosmic evolution subscribed to by the Stoic school of Greek philosophy (Khoury et al, 2001). Within this model, it is observed that inflation, even though it has been a highly successful theory, has been unable to connect to the emerging theories of quantum gravity such as M-theory. The inconsistencies between theorized and observed values in the structure of the observable universe are explained by the energy level and circumstances of the collision.

Within the Ekpyrotic universe model, the initial impetus that is thought to have caused an adjacent brane to collide with the one which contains our universe is caused by the development of an attractive force between these branes. This force is believed to be generated by quantum fluctuations in the bulk space. This effect illustrates the impact that events on the smallest scale can have on the largest scales theorized.

Dave Smith

Summary

Collectively, the concept of parallel universes has gained increasing credibility among physicists as explaining many of the unanswered questions both in quantum mechanics and in larger scale cosmology. Several models propose that when an observation is made which freezes a quantum state, or an action occurs to the preclusion of other actions, all states and actions are considered to have taken place in parallel universes. Other models explain the origin and evolution of the universe on a cosmological scale.

Dissatisfaction with the state vector collapse model proposed in the Copenhagen interpretation of quantum mechanics caused Hugh Everett to formulate the relative state interpretation in 1957. Although his work was not widely accepted, through the efforts of Bryce DeWitt, it gained popularity in the 1970s as the many worlds model.

In subsequent decades, others such as Max Tegmark and David Deutsch continued to expand Everett's model. Both have also investigated models based on the universe as an informational and mathematical structure as well. The example of quantum computing has been used as part of this ongoing work to study how information flow occurs at a larger scale.

Alan Guth proposed the inflationary model of the universe in 1981 based on his research on the big bang. Although portions of Guth's theory were found to be inaccurate, Andre Linde was inspired by it, and used the valid portions of the earlier work as the basis for his own chaotic inflation theory. This model explained the rapid growth of portions of the early universe through interactions with scalar fields which prevented energy loss by the expanding matter.

The universes formed under Linde's model are fractal in nature, exhibiting a similarity of form at any scale of observation. Benoit Mandelbrot coined the name for this form of iterative self-similar geometry, which can be observed in a number of naturally occurring structures such as coastlines and circulatory systems.

The Ekpyrotic universe theory draws on M-theory rather than on prior quantum mechanical models. It states that the event which initiated the formation of the universe which we inhabit occurred when two adjacent four-dimensional branes moving in five-dimensional space collided.

All of these models illustrate the effect that events at the quantum level can have on larger scales, whether at the level experienced directly by mankind, or at the size of the entire conceivable collection of universe volumes. The next chapter examines the ways in which this micro scale action can cause profound changes based on the initial conditions of a system. Through the principle of chaos, the smallest ripples can create the largest of waves.

Chapter 6
Chaos: Strange and Attractive

The system of the 'universe as a whole' is such that quite small errors in the initial conditions can have an overwhelming effect at a later time. The displacement of a single electron by a billionth of a centimetre at one moment might make the difference between a man being killed by an avalanche a year later, or escaping.

– Alan Turing

Alan Turing wrote the statement above in his revolutionary paper *Computing Machinery and Intelligence* in 1950. He was specifying that the computing machines that he was proposing must not exhibit this effect; rather they must be more like the model described by the Marquis de Laplace and exhibit a great degree of future predictability based upon a present state (Turing, 1950). This is known as a deterministic system, and it was discussed briefly in chapter three. Although at the quantum level, events cannot be predicted with complete certainty, many larger and more complex systems are expected to follow logical rules. This is true in magic as well as in the field of scientific enquiry. As Aleister Crowley (1929) famously stated in his book *Magick in Theory and Practice*:

> *In this book it is spoken of the Sephiroth, and the Paths, of Spirits and Conjurations; of Gods, Spheres, Planes, and many other things which may or may not exist. It is immaterial whether they exist or not. By doing certain things certain results follow; students are most earnestly warned against attributing objective reality or philosophic validity to any of them.*

This passage contains a principle which is important in many systems of magic, including quantum sorcery:

results follow actions. But even in relatively simple systems, chaotic effects can cause results to differ vastly from those that are expected.

Determinism is not a simple concept to grasp. Even within a system or function that is predictable through many iterations, irregularities frequently emerge as time passes. This is reflected mathematically by unknown digits far to the right of the decimal point working their way to the left as the result of each pass through the function is fed back into it to determine the next value. When these digits become close enough to the decimal point, their values can come to dominate the system and cause complete unpredictability. This effect is known as deterministic chaos, as it arises even in the presence of strict rules of causality (Schroeder, 1991).

In this chapter, I explore chaos theory, the study of apparently random, recurring behaviour in otherwise deterministic systems. This topic also includes the effect mentioned by Turing above, that of sensitivity to the initial conditions of the system, and how slight changes are magnified and propagated over time via feedback. Collectively, these effects act as a double-edged sword to a sorcerer, being both a mechanism by which desired changes can be manifest, and a force which can cause magical operations to go awry if not properly constructed. As with prior chapters, I provide a brief technical background of the development of the discipline of chaos theory to facilitate a greater understanding of its principles. Any magical operation, no matter how well-planned is subject to random and unexpected events. Understanding how and why this happens can help foster a mindset that is better able to cope with, and possibly counteract this effect when it occurs.

I also examine some of the types of systems which are subject to chaotic effects, how these effects are modelled for study, and how it is possible to influence chaotic systems through external means. This process has profound implications for the mechanism upon which quantum sorcery is based. It is my belief that physical events which have been experimentally verified in a purely scientific setting provide a rich source of material for inspiring magical operations.

Unexpected Disorder

Although much of the material that constitutes chaos theory was produced in the 1960s and 1970s, the origins of the theory date back to the end of the 19th century. In 1860, James Clerk Maxwell noted that collisions between molecules in gasses could cause a progressive amplification of changes resulting in randomness at the microscopic level (Wolfram, 2002). Thirty years later, Jules Henri Poincaré was working with what is known as the three-body problem. This problem attempts to describe the motion and behaviour of three bodies interacting gravitationally in space, such as satellites orbiting a planet or a planet orbiting in the plane of a pair of stars. Poincaré noted that even very slight changes in the values he was using for mass, velocity, and initial position caused sometimes catastrophic results when projected forward in time compared to the stable trajectories achieved by bodies modelled with prior values. He summarized this effect in his 1908 book *Science and Method*: "It may happen that small differences in the initial conditions produce very great ones in the final phenomena. A small error in the former will produce an enormous error in the latter. Prediction becomes impossible." Systems in which this process occurs are often referred to as being *stochastic*, from the Greek word for "guess."

Part of the difficulty in solving the three-body problem arises from the *nonlinear* relationship between the terms in its equations. This means that unlike linear functions, in which future results can be easily deduced from those generated by prior solutions, that earlier results cannot be assumed to have any predictive value on those in the future. Each result must be solved for individually. Nonlinear equations are characterized by terms which are being raised to an exponential power, such as squaring or cubing them. In this case, gravity is the responsible term, as the strength of attraction between two masses is inversely proportional to the square of their distance.

After Poincaré, a number of mathematicians and physicists including Andrei Kolmogorov and George Birkhoff did work with nonlinear equations, but it was not until computers were used to analyse these functions that interest in them widened greatly. Edward Lorenz, a meteorologist at the Massachusetts Institute of Technology began to use a digital computer to model atmospheric systems in 1960. He discovered that by truncating a value having six decimal places down to only three caused a divergence in modelled behaviour after being projected forward only a few months. He wrote about his findings in a 1963 paper, *Deterministic Nonperiodic Flow*.

One of the notable features of the paper was the graphic representation of the results of the oscillating behaviour of the model weather system. When graphed in *phase space*, a multi-dimensional representation of values over time, the results produced a double-looping graph which has been compared to a twisted infinity or a butterfly's wings. This figure has come to be known as the *Lorenz attractor*. I will cover both phase space and attractors in greater detail later in this chapter.

Lorenz's paper was printed in the *Journal of Atmospheric Sciences* and was unfortunately not widely read by many mathematicians or physicists. It was only later when mathematician James Yorke was shown the paper by a colleague who worked with fluid dynamics that Lorenz's work began to be more widely known. Yorke co-wrote a paper in 1975, *Period Three Implies Chaos*, to help spread the ideas which Lorenz had discovered. This was the paper that first associated the name of chaos with the study of deterministic disorder (Gleick, 1987). Three years prior to this, Lorenz himself coined another phrase which is widely associated with this field. At the December 1972 meeting of the American Association for the Advancement of Science, he presented a talk titled *Predictability: Does the Flap of a Butterfly's Wings in Brazil set off a Tornado in Texas?* Thus *the butterfly effect* was born.

Sensitivity to Initial Conditions

A more widely used term for the butterfly effect is *sensitivity to initial conditions*. As is implied, this state describes systems whose behaviour patterns diverge at some point after making slight alterations to their starting values. This effect of nonlinearity appears in both Poincaré's three-body research and in Lorenz's atmospheric modelling and has been found unexpectedly in other areas of research as well.

Ironically, Lorenz was not the first to associate this effect with a butterfly, although in a different context. In 1952, Science Fiction author Ray Bradbury wrote the short story *A Sound of Thunder*. In it, he used the death of a butterfly during a time traveling safari to illustrate the profound effects that such a small event in the far distant past could have on the present day. In this case, the entire political climate of the United States was changed from progressive to totalitarian.

Bradbury's story is a classic example of this effect in action.

In analysing the unexpected results in the three-body problem, Poincaré came to realise that initial conditions of all variables in a system would have to be determined to infinite precision in order to eliminate the effects that he was observing. Even with the massive amounts of computer processing power and extremely accurate instrumentation available to modern researchers, this is still not possible with regard to studying real world phenomena. An unknown value at the millionth decimal place can still lead to chaotic behaviour at a later point in the system.

The Lorentz model, named for the Dutch physicist Hendrik Lorentz, illustrates this effect. It involves a small hard sphere of known trajectory bouncing off larger, randomly distributed spheres in an enclosed region. If any uncertainty is introduced into the system, no matter how small, the probability of locating the small sphere at any location in the region becomes uniform.

In his modelling, Edward Lorenz ultimately arrived at the same conclusion as Poincaré. He wrote in the conclusion to *Deterministic Nonperiodic Flow* (1963):

> ...*prediction of the sufficiently distant future is impossible by any method, unless the present conditions are known exactly. In view of the inevitable inaccuracy and incompleteness of weather observations, precise very-long-range forecasting would seem to be non-existent.*

Lorenz was unable to give a strict definition of exactly how long "very-long-range" might be, whether days or centuries. He suggested comparing pairs of numerical solutions which had nearly identical initial conditions.

Looking for the point at which the graphs diverged from one another would give a general indication of the forward-looking capability of a given model.

The process that Lorenz referred to for measuring the divergence of trajectories over time is known as the *Lyapunov exponent* for Russian mathematician Aleksandr Lyapunov. A simplified description of this process for purposes of illustration is that it is a function which calculates the ratio of two different solutions to a function and generates a number which indicates whether or not the trajectories generated from that function diverge. If the trajectories do not diverge, the Lyapunov exponent will be zero.

The graphing of most functions takes place on the two-dimensional X-Y axis plane which is familiar to most students of geometry or algebra. If the X-axis represents the passage of time, and the Y-axis the value of the function at that point in time, such a graph is known as a *time series*. This structure is useful for showing the progression of a single value but limiting in the case of complex systems which are dependent upon multiple variables. In these cases, it is often more useful to rely on phase space for graphing results.

The ultimate example of an emerging system that is subject to sensitivity to initial conditions is the Universe itself. The states of matter and energy when it was infinitesimal and dense, prior to expansion, were foundational to the states that we now find nearly 14 billion years later.

Phase Space and Attractors

As I touched on previously, phase space is a multi-dimensional representation of values over time. Rather than containing a single variable which changes over time as in a time series, this method of modelling represents one dimension for each variable in a dynamic system. The advantage that this type of modelling provides is that the complete state of the system at any point in time can be represented as a point in the phase space. This allows the possible development of patterns in the system to be more easily visualised. Just as graphing a point on the X and Y axes requires two coordinates; every point in a phase space containing any number of dimensions N can likewise be specified by its set of N coordinates.

In order to display his results, which consisted of three variables representing convective motion in the air mass, the temperature difference between ascending and descending air currents, and the degree to which the temperature profile was distorted away from a linear norm, Edward Lorenz used a phase space. When each result representing the state of the system at a given point in time was placed into this graph, the resulting trajectories never repeat themselves exactly, and in each branch of the loop they orbit around an empty centre which Lorenz designated as representing stable convection. As the results of each iteration are graphed, the trajectories oscillate back and forth creating the double-loop structure of the Lorenz Attractor.

In general, *attractors* represent a state of stability into which dynamic systems tend to settle into at some point in their development. In typical systems, trajectories formed in phase space will eventually be so similar that a single one can be selected to represent the overall character of the system. This representative trajectory is likely the attractor. Most attractors resemble either single points in phase space, also known as steady-state, or a closed loop. The former indicates that nothing is happening in the system, and the latter represents periodic motion, a pattern which repeats cyclically over time.

The attractor that Lorenz discovered is different than those typically observed in dynamic systems. The behaviour that produces it is nonperiodic, and its trajectories in phase space are similar, but never identically repeat. This is one of the first examples identified of what is known as a *strange attractor*. David Ruelle and Floris Takens coined this term in their 1971 paper *On the Nature of Turbulence* to describe the strange geometry of the attractors produced by turbulent fluid systems. As trajectories in the phase space of the Lorenz attractor progress, points which were in close proximity to one another initially diverge over time. They follow similar courses until the slight differences in their initial conditions cause one trajectory to follow one branch of the loop structure, while the other continues on the path that both were apparently going to follow. This behaviour is characteristic of strange attractors in general.

A similar effect to the divergence of trajectories in a strange attractor is the phenomenon of *bifurcation*. This is when one or more variables which dictate a trajectory reach a certain threshold and cause that trajectory to randomly take one of two paths. Most instances of bifurcation occur in dynamic systems that are far from equilibrium (Prigogene and Stengers, 1984). Through this process, previously stable attractors can re-form into strange attractors. Some examples of this effect are the change of behaviour in water running from a spigot as the flow rate is increased, and the change that a column of smoke rising from a cigarette as it goes from smooth, or *laminar* flow to a state of turbulence.

The exact point at which the type of flow, and hence the attractor will change, is very difficult to calculate, even with massive computer resources. Although bifurcation is a stochastic process, there is experimental evidence that some systems, such as chemical reactions which are subject to bifurcation, can be influenced by the application of gravitational or electromagnetic fields (Prigogene and Stengers).

Feedback and Cascades

Not all instability within a system is the result of initial conditions. The introduction of uncertainty into a system at any given point during its development is also a possibility. In this case, even if such disturbances are small and isolated within a single variable of the system, they can magnify over time into larger perturbations which will affect the whole system.

This effect is especially common in iterative systems in which each new state is dependent on a previous state. As small variations in initial conditions are fed back into subsequent iterations within a system, the variation increases, and the process, if no compensation is made, will continue to pull the system into a chaotic state. This process is known as feedback. One familiar form of this effect is when a microphone or electric guitar feeds it own output back into its own amplifier, creating a wailing, high-pitched scream.

The effect of feedback is also evident in the cycles of populations. Biologist Robert May was performing research on predator-prey relationships when he discovered that nonlinear feedback in the environment caused pseudo-random changes in population. If the population of a species increases during one year, they will deplete the available food supply causing many to starve to death. The subsequent year reflects a return to a smaller population. Any species which preys upon the one being studied are also affected, as will any further up the food chain, creating what May referred to as a "biological many-body problem" (May, 1991).

While modelling population dynamics mathematically, May discovered that the function he used to describe them was subject to bifurcation when the population growth rate passed a certain threshold. This accurately replicated the oscillation between successive years of alternating large and small physical populations.

When a perturbation or feedback causes effects which propagate across scales, from smaller systems up into larger systems, the process is often referred to as a *cascade*. This effect can also be viewed as the physical manifestation of a system responding to changes in its initial conditions. The flap of a butterfly's wings potentially causing tornados a year later elsewhere in the world is a popular and graphic illustration of this effect. Another example is tossing a ping-pong ball into a room full of set mouse traps. When one springs, it causes a cascading ripple of springing traps which radiates outward from it.

In my prior discussion of the Level 2 parallel universe, I compared the creation of cascading effects at the quantum scale to Linde's theory of eternal inflation. This is in reference to the quotation by Alan Turing at the beginning of this chapter. By influencing and hence displacing a single electron by a billionth of a centimetre, a cascade can be caused that can affect events on the macro scale. One way in which an electron can be so influenced is by collisions with other fundamental particles, such as photons.

It is possible that a perturbation caused by the change in

electron momentum could alter the paths of other particles, and those so altered could do likewise, thus providing the start of a cascade which propagates upward in scale through an unknown number of interactions as atoms, molecules and eventually the macro scale of the world of human interaction are affected.

Entropy and the Arrow of Time

The very nature of dynamic systems is that they evolve over time. Time was largely ignored in Newton's original physics, but as the laws of thermodynamics began to be understood, it became apparent that although many physical laws are time reversible, such as electricity, magnetism, and gravitation, not all are. The second law of thermodynamics states that certain occurrences, such as the generation of heat by friction, among others, are irreversible (Planck, in Ferris, 1991). In any process in which energy is transferred, particularly as heat, some degree of the energy involved in the transfer will always be lost. In 1865, Rudolf Clausius introduced this concept as *entropy*.

Entropy is envisioned as a quantity which always increases in a system due to heat loss. Heat is produced by the effect of random motions among particles in a system, so the measure of entropy can also be interpreted as the amount of disorder in a system. Entropy always attempts to reach a maximum, which is known as the point of thermodynamic equilibrium. In theory, this equilibrium point is never actually attainable in a real physical system, due to the exchange of energy and heat with other systems, but it is the process of trying to reach this point which is perceived as time (Coveney, 1991).

The irreversibility of events, caused by an increase in

entropy is what determines that the *arrow of time* goes only in one direction, and prohibits the possibility of travel to the past. As Ilya Prigogine (1984) states:

> *An infinite entropy barrier separates possible initial conditions from prohibited ones. Because this barrier is infinite, technological progress will never be able to overcome it. We have to abandon the hope that one day we will be able to travel back into our past.*

In order to reverse time, the complete state of every particle in the physical universe at a prior time would have to be known. Even if random fluctuations at the Planck scale did not preclude this possibility, and the universe were fully deterministic in the way that Laplace had envisioned, the problem would still remain that a processing and storage mechanism capable of recording the complete state of the universe could not be housed in the information space of the universe itself.

A conclusion is then reached that within the complex system of the physical universe, the objective past cannot be revisited due to the barrier of infinite entropy, and the distant future cannot be determined due to the inability to measure initial conditions to an infinite degree of precision. Within the boundaries of a given physical universe, this leaves only the possibility of short-range predictability or determination available as an option for a sorcerer who wishes to exert their Will on the system to alter probability and cause desired outcomes to be manifest.

This conclusion does not preclude the attainment of long-term results; it only suggests that such results are the creation of short-term cascades created by direct influence. The farther out in time a magical operation reaches, the less precise control should be expected. Again, this is the question that Lorenz was faced with, what constitutes a long period of time? Only by recording the results of each magical operation, and comparing its degree of success with the time frame in which it ultimately did or did not achieve the desired end can the range of influence be determined by an individual sorcerer, if such information is of interest.

Summary

Ironically, much of what is now understood about chaotic systems emerged from the desire to predict the future. Even within deterministic dynamic systems, fluctuations and anomalies may arise which cause the system to ultimately exhibit chaotic behaviour and fail to yield expected results. This is due both to the inability to measure initial system conditions with infinite precision, and through the introduction of perturbations into the system over time. These perturbations may be the result of external forces interacting with the system, or through the magnification of minute and potentially undetectable instability within the system via the mechanism of feedback. Jules Henri Poincaré observed this in his work with three-body orbital systems, thirty years after James Clerk Maxwell first noted this behaviour while observing gas molecules.

The magnification of small changes into larger ones is due in large part to the nonlinear and iterative nature of the systems themselves. This phenomenon is known as sensitivity to initial conditions and was popularized after the discovery by Edward Lorenz that truncating long decimals in his atmospheric modelling work led to unexpected behaviour in the output of his functions. His graphic representations of these results in phase space led to what is perhaps the best-known example of a strange attractor.

Attractors are points of stability toward which chaotic systems tend to be drawn. These may demonstrate a steady state or oscillation between two or more states, or in the case of strange attractors, the trajectory of the system may be similar but never identical as it tries to reach equilibrium.

Perturbations in a micro-scale system sometimes have the potential to propagate upward in scale, causing a cascading event which can cause effects to be manifest at the macro scale. Future states of complex systems are incredibly hard to predict with a great deal of certainty, which limits prediction or influence over a system to only short ranges in time. Past system states can likewise be difficult to model and traveling back in time has been shown to be theoretically impossible due to infinite entropy barrier. Entropy is a measure of disorder in a system which results from the loss of energy through the production of heat. In all observations to date, it has proven to be irreversible and unpreventable.

This chapter has introduced several topics which become useful in fostering an understanding of both the capabilities and the limitations of what sorcery can be used to accomplish. By focusing efforts on the short term, aimed at initiating a cascade at the smallest possible scale, the greatest degree of results can be achieved without wasting effort and energy in an attempt to manipulate reality outside of the parameters of physical law.

In the next chapter I examine the roll that the human mind plays in Quantum Sorcery. As a potential holographic interface, and as a sophisticated tool for visualisation, it is in the mind that the Will first forms its designs for altering reality prior to projecting them out into the phenomenal universe.

Models of Mind and Manipulation: The Microcosm

Chapter 7
Quantifying Consciousness

It is a psychological fact that we believe we have the ability to control and modify our actions by the exercise of "will", and in practical life all sane men will assume they have this ability.

– Sir John Eccles

The roots of sorcery lie within the human desire to know and influence the future. This process is found in many cultures, regardless of their perceived level of sophistication. With sentience and self-awareness come emotional and intellectual uncertainty and the acknowledgement that mankind is often constrained by forces beyond our control or understanding. In order to alleviate these uncertainties of the human condition, our natural response is the creation of a process which will allow us some degree of control over our circumstances.

Even in the face of information-age technology and the dogma of globally organized religions, the individual desire to know and control future events has not been eliminated. Sorcery is still an alternative for those who wish to have a direct effect over the probabilities that affect their lives. As the sciences provide an increasingly coherent description of both internal and external reality, the number of tools and methods available to the sorcerer who is willing to depart from traditional definitions of magic and embrace them grows daily.

In much the same way that quantum theory shook the foundations of the physics world, a number of alternative theories for explaining human consciousness and self-awareness have caused a great deal of debate within the disciplines of psychology and neuroscience. Some of these theories have failed to gain popularity and have fallen into obscurity. Others continue to propagate, sometimes in the face of withering criticism from skeptical peers. As is often the case, the conflict between entrenched ideas and those which challenge the status quo is fierce. The question as to whether or not human consciousness can be explained within classical models of the brain, or whether the effects of quantum mechanics play a role are still being argued across a wide array of scientific disciplines.

As before, I present this brief encapsulation of ideas to provide a basic background in the subject matter. I highly encourage additional study in this area. The models discussed are only a sampling of the many theories that have been proposed to explain human consciousness. Some of these theories focus on the structure of the brain, while others emphasize the processes which take place within it.

All acts of sorcery begin as acts of desire and Will within the mind of the sorcerer. To study of the processes by which the internal functions of the brain relate to the external processes of the external world is to study the birthplace of these forces and ultimately the source of self-awareness. Although the structure of the brain has been analysed in great detail, and the functions of the various neurotransmitters, which initiate and control the propagation of impulses throughout the brain, have been cataloged, the ultimate nature of consciousness and sentience has still not been explained satisfactorily.

Brain Waves

Building on research performed in the late 19th century by British physician Richard Caton, German psychiatrist Hans Berger documented the electrical nature of the human brain in 1924. While researching electric potential in biological cells, he observed that the brain in particular generates measurable and predictable electric activity. He named his discovery *alpha waves*. These typically range in frequency from 8.5 to 12 Hertz, or cycles per second. Although their signal was relatively weak, Berger discovered that they could be amplified in order to produce *electroencephalograms*, which are graphic representations of the waves.

Subsequent investigations in the 1930s by W. Grey Walter revealed a range of wave forms, including the .5 to 4 Hz *delta* waves produced in deep sleep, the 4.5 to 8 Hz *theta* waves which are characteristic of states of drowsiness or trance, the 12 to 30 Hz *beta* waves which are typical of normal consciousness, and *gamma* waves which have a frequency of 30 to 80 Hz or higher, and are typically indicative of high levels of mental activity and perception. Walter also first detected the *contingent negative variation*, which is a drop in the electrical activity in the frontal lobe of the brain which precedes the self-awareness of physical movement. The implication of this effect is that the conscious mind is only notified of the nervous system's intention to act after the decision has already been made by other processes in the brain.

One of the effects that Walter discovered was that the frequency of brain waves could be influenced with using external stimuli. His experiments used a strobe light, and he found that the waves would adjust to match the frequency of the light pulses. This occurs through wave processes that will be described in the next chapter. The effect of flickering light to induce altered states of consciousness had been recorded since at least the second century, but until Walter's work, it was unknown exactly why this occurred.

Brion Gysin is credited with popularizing the use of this principle via the *dream machine* in the early 1960s. Based on discussions with Gysin and an awareness of Walter's work, Ian Sommerville first built a prototype in 1960. Over the next year, Gysin experimented with his own version of the machine. It consisted of a light source in a rotating cylinder into which patterns of holes were cut. As the cylinder turned, it produced light flashes intended to induce an alpha wave pattern in the brain of the observer. A multitude of devices are now available which perform the same function as the dream machine. Some of these use small individual flashing lights, and others also include sound to assist in inducing the desired state of mind. Users of these devices have reported every type of result, from nothing at all to transcendental visions.

The Holonomic Brain

Karl Pribram doesn't believe that the mind exists at all as a physical entity. In a 1998 interview, he stated: "I don't like the term the mind, because it reifies – that means it makes a thing of – something that's a process. We pay attention, we see, we hear. Those are all mental processes, mental activities. But there isn't a thing called the mind" (Mishlove, 1998). Pribram has been an important researcher in the field of neuropsychology and is known for his work in defining the role and structure of the limbic system in the brain. However, despite his strong credentials, his theory of the *holonomic brain* (from the Greek roots for whole and management) has earned him notoriety both within and outside of the field that he has contributed to so much.

In 1946, Pribram began a two-year stint working with neuropsychologist Karl Lashely. Since the 1920s, Lashely had been performing studies with rats in an attempt to determine where memories of trained behaviour were stored in the brain. What he discovered was that regardless of which portion of the brain he removed, the rats still retained the memory of their training. Lashely's findings convinced Pribram that in contrast to the popular theory of the time that memories, encoded in units known as *engrams*, are stored in a discrete location within the brain, that memories must instead be distributed throughout the structure of the brain. Unfortunately, at that time, there was no known mechanism which could explain this theory.

It was not until Pribram was exposed to the work of mathematician Dennis Gabor, the inventor of the hologram that a theoretical framework for his idea began to develop. As I discussed in chapter four, a hologram is a three-dimensional image produced by recording the interference patterns of laser light which has been split. One of the split beams is reflected off an object onto a photographic plate, while the other segment of the split beam is reflected directly onto the plate. The resulting image is entirely contained in every region of the plate. There is no one-to-one correlation between spatial points of the image and those of the object.

Pribram realised that this phenomenon very closely paralleled the results that Lashley had observed. Sensory input, converted to memory, seems to be stored over a wide region of the brain's structure through the natural application of a *spread function*. This type of function, also known as a *Fourier transformation* in honour of French mathematician Jean Baptiste Joseph Fourier, can be used to convert spatial coordinates into frequencies. When memories are accessed, the process is reversed within the brain, creating an internal reconstruction of the information which has been encoded by the senses.

Dave Smith

Conscious awareness is explained within this model as an effect of this reconstruction process.

This method of encoding and retrieving sensory information relies on the electrochemical nature of the brain, as well as the fractal network of neurons, the nerve cells in the brain. Electrical impulses lasting approximately one one-thousandth of a second continually travel throughout this network, which consists of approximately 10^{11} cells (Hole, 1984). Although some researchers investigating this model have focused on standing waves in the brain, Pribram focused instead on the greater neural network as a whole, considering the relationship between the structure and the electrical impulses it carries as a single system. He theorized that nerve impulses create a matrix of interference patterns, analogous to those of a holographic image on a photographic plate. It is through these interference patterns that consciousness is manifest and memories are created and accessed. I discuss this in greater in a later chapter, Pribram's consciousness model is closely related to David Bohm's theory of the implicate order, that space and time are enfolded, and it is through the unfolding of these phenomena that reality is manifest.

This model has had a number of critics who have attempted to refute it, but in at least one notable case, such an attempt led to a reversal of belief. American neuroscientist Paul Pietsch tried to disprove Lashley and Pribram's findings in a study which included removing segments of the brains of salamanders. Pietsch referred to these as "shufflebrain" experiments. Rather than disproving the theory, his results confirmed the earlier findings, and he became a believer in the new model. He discovered that not only are the memories of learned behaviours spread throughout the structure of the brain, but that by transplanting portions of brains between different amphibians, that behaviour patterns taught to the brain donor are inherited by the recipient, although with some loss of clarity (Pietsch).

The ability of the brain to reconstruct memories in the case of severe damage or even missing significant portions of its physical structure is a strong argument for the validity of this model of memory and consciousness, but it is still not accepted by the majority of neuroscientists. One development that has possibly leant some credence to it is the greater understanding of how the production and comprehension of language is manifest. Once thought to be confined primarily to two small parts of the brain, *Broca's area* and *Wernicke's area*, it has been determined that language is distributed throughout many regions (Huth et al, 2016).

The Human Biocomputer

American physician and neuroscientist John Lilly believed that the human brain was a biocomputer, and that almost all learned conscious and subconscious behaviour patterns, or *programs*, could be altered. As I briefly touched on in chapter two, he referred to this process as metaprogramming. Lilly first conceived the idea of metaprogramming in 1949, when he was first introduced to the principles of computer software design. Based on his pioneering work in mapping the structure of the brain, he realised the parallels between the disciplines, and began to explore and define his new model.

In 1954, in ongoing research to learn how the brain would respond to a complete lack of external stimuli, Lilly developed the first isolation tank. Through the use of this device, and the sensory deprivation it provided, he was able to confirm that the human brain remained active and alert, and even that altered states of consciousness were easier to reach. From 1964 through 1966, Lilly expanded his research by adding the use of LSD to his sessions in the isolation tank. The results of this work were summarized in the 1967 book *Programming and Metaprogramming in the Human Biocomputer*. Later in the course of his experimentation, Lilly added ketamine to the regimen of consciousness-expanding substances in his work and reported his findings in part through his 1978 autobiography *The Scientist*. It is likely that far more people are aware of the fictional adaptation of Lilly's work than the actuality, as it was the basis for the 1978 novel and 1980 film *Altered States*.

The concept of metaprogramming is a shortcut to a related collection of processes. Lilly (1972) wrote that:

> *When one learns to learn, one is making models, using symbols, analogizing, making metaphors, in short, inventing and using language, mathematics, art, politics, business, etc...To avoid the necessity of repeating learning to learn, symbols, metaphors, models each time, I symbolize the underlying idea in these operations as metaprogramming.*

From the hundreds of thousands of programs running in a brain, a fluid set of thousands of metaprograms can emerge. From this subset, one or more constructs arise which guide and control the hierarchy below it. These are known as *self metaprogrammers* and are associated with the "I" or "me" of a self-aware brain.

Not all programs are the same. Some, such as eating, sex, fear, pain, and avoidance are entrenched at the biological level, and are almost impossible to alter. Other programs are acquired throughout a life-long process of interaction with the environment, and with other sentient organisms. The sum of all programs and metaprograms of a biocomputer comprise the mind. It is analogous to software, while the brain itself is the hardware upon which the collection runs (Lilly).

Lilly's consciousness model describes the functional behaviour of the brain, and how an individual may take the initiative to re-program their behaviour patterns. It does not concern itself more than peripherally with the physical structure of the brain. Despite that fact that some of Lilly's best known research involved the detailed mapping of portions of the brain, he later stated in an interview that "I gave up long ago trying to figure out how the brain works because it's so immense and so complex." He also refutes the model of memory storage espoused by Pribram and his supporters such as Rupert Sheldrake as being an over-simplification (Brown and Novick, 1991).

Like Karl Pribram, John Lilly was often thought within the neuroscientific community to be a brilliant scientist who lost his way and strayed into metaphysics. Lilly's willingness to use himself as an experimental subject for studying the effects of LSD, ketamine, and PCP upon self-awareness and the self-programming of consciousness kept most of his later research out of professional journals, as well as generating concern among some of his colleagues. In one of his experiences on LSD, he experienced a state of consciousness in which he become aware of all possible paths in space-time which could be taken from that moment. He referred to this state as *alternity* (Brown and Novick). This concept closely parallels the quantum state of superposition, and the course actually taken would similarly parallel the process of decoherence at the quantum level.

Dave Smith

The essence of John Lilly's model is summed up in a statement which also illustrates the applicability of his work to the toolkit of a sorcerer:

> *In the province of the mind, what one believes to be true is true or becomes true, within certain limits to be found experientially and experimentally. These limits are further beliefs to be transcended. In the mind, there are no limits (Lilly).*

The potency of this system for causing change within the self is unquestionable, but as I discussed in chapter two, the risks are also great. Sensory deprivation on its own, without the addition of psychoactive substances, is still a useful method for introspection and meditation, and is certainly a less risky starting point for anyone interested in trying to follow the trail that Lilly blazed.

Orchestrated Objective Reduction

Possibly the most heated debates about the possible interaction of quantum mechanics and consciousness have resulted from the model developed by British physicist Roger Penrose and American physician Stuart Hameroff, orchestrated objective reduction. This theory states that if a quantum wave function in a state of superposition avoids the process of decoherence (i.e. the collapse of its state vector), assumedly by avoiding interactions with a surrounding environment, that eventually an objective threshold for collapse, or reduction, is reached. This very process is thought to occur within structures known as *microtubules* which are part of the cytoskeleton, or outer shell of neurons. Hameroff and Penrose suggest that when this reduction occurs, a conscious event is generated (Niemark, 2003).

Microtubules are hollow tubular structures of various lengths and approximately 2.5 x 10^{-9} meters in diameter built out of the protein *tubulin*. The individual tubulin molecules are dynamic, and the microtubules are in a constant state of assembly and disassembly. The movement of individual tubulin components within their framework is capable of causing wavelike signals which travel along the larger tubular structures. The proposed relationship of this action to quantum events is described in a paper by Hameroff and Penrose (1996):

> *We envisage that conformational states of microtubule subunits (tubulins) are coupled to internal quantum events, and cooperatively interact (compute) with other tubulins. We further assume that macroscopic coherent superposition of quantum-coupled tubulin conformational states occurs throughout significant brain volumes and provides the global binding essential to consciousness. A wave function might avoid decoherence for as long as 500 milliseconds before the threshold required for self-orchestrated reduction is reached.*

Critics of this theory offer a number of arguments refuting the possibility that a state of superposition in a quantum event can be sustained in the brain. They point out that the environment of the brain is not well-suited to the state of isolation that is required for a quantum system to remain in this state. Hameroff in response to this attack has proposed that the structure of the cell material is capable of shielding the microtubules from interacting with the heat of the brain long enough to build up to the orchestration threshold (Woolf and Hameroff, 2001).

One of the prominent physicists who found fault with the "Orch OR" model is Max Tegmark, whose work with the many worlds theory was discussed in chapter five. His argument against quantum effects in the brain are based on his calculations of how long it would take for a decoherence event to occur in microtubules and neurons. His results, which range from 10^{-13} to 10^{-20} seconds, are far shorter than the 10^{-3} timeframe indicated by Hameroff and Penrose, and thus he has concluded that such states collapse too quickly to be responsible for generating consciousness (Tegmark, 1999).

Another detractor of the theory, Victor Stenger, supports the theory that the brain is bound by the rules of classical physics rather than quantum mechanics. He suggests that the brain evolved in the way that it did, and at the structural scale that it did, specifically in order to avoid the uncertainty inherent at the quantum scale. As he observes, "Certainly quantum mechanics is needed to understand the atoms in the brain. But it is also needed to explain the atoms in a rock, and this implies nothing about rock consciousness" (Stenger, 1996).

The camps of supporters and opponents of "Orch OR" continue to spar, but in general the theory is still not widely accepted. This does not mean that the model might not ultimately be adopted, but science is frequently a strong bastion of consensus reality, and such acceptance would probably require one or more as of yet unmade supporting discoveries before critics of the theory acquiesce.

The Bose-Einstein Condensate Model

Another theory which is based on quantum mechanics is the Bose-Einstein condensate model proposed by Danah Zohar. This theory states that the coherent emission of biologically generated energy (which I'll discuss in depth in a later chapter) from neurons in a *condensed phase* quantum state is the basis for consciousness (Zohar, 1990). The condensed phase state, initially theorized by Satyendra Bose and later formalized by Albert Einstein describes a phase of matter which occurs when a gas is cooled to near absolute zero, the point at which all molecular motion stops. The result suggests that all of the particles in the condensate share the same quantum state, and that the waveforms of all of the particles are in phase.

This theory follows the work of German physicist Herbert Fröhlich who had performed research on electric potentials in biological membranes in the late 1960s. He discovered that some such structures, when subjected to a high enough rate of energy input by their surrounding metabolism, will emit a coherent electrical field which is very similar to a Bose-Einstein condensate, although at environmentally normal metabolic temperatures (Fröhlich, 1988). This is typically referred to as a *pumped system*.

Zohar suggests that the electrical signals transmitted across neuron boundaries stimulate the emission of photons from the neuron cell walls. The increase in signal frequency that results from adjacent neurons propagating the impulses through the neural network eventually reaches a critical level which causes a state of coherent oscillation among the molecules in the cellular membrane. This coherent oscillation creates the Bose-Einstein condensate as predicted by Fröhlich. This unified field is believed to be the basis for the ground state of consciousness.

Zohar further speculates that the instantaneous changes in the number of molecules contained in the neuronal condensate accounts for the relative strength of consciousness. This quantity could be affected by factors such as blood sugar levels, drugs, and the intensity of sensory stimuli which are being processed by the brain at any particular moment. This fluctuation in condensate field intensity is proposed as the underlying cause of the different brain wave patterns first observed by Berger and Walter.

This model is very similar to an earlier form of Penrose and Hameroff's "Orch OR" model, and it has been subject to some of the same objections from those who doubt that a state of coherence can be maintained in the brain. In general, less acerbic criticism has been brought to bear against Zohar's ideas, possibly because she has maintained a higher degree of abstraction in her theory and has relied upon fewer departures from the classical model than have Penrose and Hameroff. Biologist Jonathan Edwards, although critical of most existing quantum consciousness theories in general, suggests that there is a greater possibility of coherence in the larger structure of a cellular membrane, as its structure is capable of supporting a more complex wave pattern than the filament-like microtubules could (Edwards, 2005).

Summary

With self-awareness comes the desire for control over our environment and circumstances. The development of sorcery as a system to provide such control through the ability to know and influence future events is a natural response to this desire.

Given that all works of sorcery begin as conscious acts of the Will, an awareness of the processes from which consciousness is thought to originate is conducive to a better understanding of where sorcery begins, as a human mental process.

Hans Berger was the first researcher to document the electrical nature of the human brain. His discovery of the alpha brain wave pattern and subsequent recording of it via electroencephalography inspired W. Grey Walter to further explore the entire continuum of electrical activity of the brain in its various states of rest or activity. His experimentation with the regulation of these states through flashing lights led Ian Sommerville and Brion Gysin to construct the dream machine, a device which was intended for individuals to regulate their own brain wave patterns for relaxation and visualisation.

Karl Pribram's holonomic brain theory suggests that conscious awareness is the result of the mind reconstructing information which it has stored holographically throughout its structure. The electrical impulses which travel throughout the neural network create an interference pattern which acts as the means of information storage and retrieval. Pribram first conceived of this theory after working with Karl Lashely in his ultimately unsuccessful attempts to locate the engram, a proposed unit of memory storage within the brain. Attempts to disprove this theory by Paul Pietsch resulted instead in its validation, and in Pietsch's conversion to a supporter of the new paradigm.

John Lilly's work focused more on the processes through which the brain functions rather than on its physical structure. He believed the brain is a biocomputer, and that patterns of conscious and subconscious behaviour are in fact programs which can be modified through the use of altered states and psychoactive substances. In addition to basic self-programming through the manipulation of symbols, Lilly also conceived of a more abstract system of modifying the self via the process of metaprogramming. This system encapsulates all of the aspects of self-programming into a framework which avoids the limitations of normal informational structures and allows the direct addressing of the various active aspects of the self.

In one of his experiments with LSD, Lilly reported that he achieved a state of consciousness which he called alternity. This is analogous to the state of quantum superposition. From this point of view, the parallel could be extended such that when an actual pathway through space-time is selected, such an act would compare to decoherence and the collapse of the quantum wave function.

Roger Penrose and Stuart Hameroff theorized that consciousness is a result of the collapse of the state vectors of quantum systems in microscopic structures in the brain. Their orchestrated objective reduction model states that quantum wave functions can remain in a state of superposition for up to 500 milliseconds while shielded from interaction within the microtubules which are part of the outer structure of neurons. This theory has been contested by a number of other physicists.

A similar but more abstract quantum consciousness model has been proposed by Danah Zohar. Her Bose-Einstein condensate model relies on the principle of the Fröhlich pumped system, and states that neurons receive enough energy from the electrochemical propagation of impulses to establish a coherent field which she believes to be the basis for the ground state of consciousness. The number of molecules which contribute to the field determines the relative strength of the consciousness created. This theory has not been attacked by opponents with the same vigour as the "Orch OR" model has.

At the current level of capability in the scientific analysis of intangible phenomenon such as consciousness as a process, no one theory has been able to surpass the others to become dominant. The possibility remains that every single one of the models ever created could simply be wrong. Until more information on exactly how the process works is discovered, the issue remains a matter of metaphysical and scientific debate and consensus. Fortunately, a sorcerer is not constrained by consensus, and in the absence of a dominant paradigm is free to choose whichever one is most advantageous to his or her work.

A belief in the existence of magic does not require an understanding of the process by which desires formed within an individual consciousness might be propagated outward any more than the ability to drive a car requires knowledge of the principles of an internal combustion engine. There is however both a certain feeling of satisfaction and a greater degree of appreciation for the activity which can be gained from an understanding of the underlying mechanism.

In this case, having some concept of how the self originates, and how it relates to that which is not the self can be a useful tool for understanding how reality may be manipulated in both the subjective and phenomenal worlds. When the psychic censor is presented with plausible explanations for how otherwise "impossible" actions are to be carried out, it is less likely to try and inhibit these actions.

Chapter 8
Resonance and Reality

I — I in the widest meaning of the word, that is to say, every conscious mind that has ever said or felt 'I' — am the person, if any, who controls the 'motion of the atoms' according to the Laws of Nature.

– Erwin Schrödinger

I have introduced several models which attempt to explain how the universe was formed, as well as several theories on how consciousness occurs. The next step is to seek a method by which the desired results formulated in the mind can be created in the outer world. To a large degree, this depends on which paradigms are being embraced by the sorcerer to explain the inner and outer worlds, but some methods are applicable regardless of which models are believed to best represent reality. The focus of this chapter is on those models which describe the interaction of mind and matter through wave actions which allow the transmission of experience and information between human consciousness and the larger environment.

In chapter one, I discussed sympathetic magic, which is accomplished by performing an action on a representation of an object, in the expectation that the action will also be manifest on the actual object. This effect is accomplished by creating a *magical link* between the object and its simulacrum. This link can be created through a variety of ways. If working with an entity which has a specific symbol or logo associated with it, using this to create the link can be highly effective. This works whether the entity in question is believed to be a supernatural entity, or something more mundane such as a corporation or product brand.

In several traditional forms of magic, the inclusion of bodily artifacts such as hair, nail clippings, or bodily fluids are obtained, and then used to create a link between a person and their simulacrum by incorporating them into its construction. Such items already have an inherent physical connection to a person, which makes a magical connection that much easier to establish. This effect in general is a part of a larger set of widely used principles known as the laws of *similarity* and *contagion*. Essentially these laws boil down to the beliefs that like attracts or effects like, and that an item which is a part of, or has been in contact with, another object takes on some of that other object's properties.

Besides the use of constructed replicas and other physical artifacts, the magical link can also be used on a more abstract level. The visualisation of a particular situation that is desired can be created either purely through mental visualisations, or through a combination of physical media. This can be via sound recordings, written statements, video or photo collages, etc. The concept is to create a micro scale reality that can be used by the sorcerer to propagate into the macro scale.

As in all endeavours which involve manipulating possibility and probability, this does not work every time. This can be for any number of reasons. Sometimes this is due to hidden parameters that are affecting the situation and sometimes the possibility of a situation is simply too remote to manipulate into being with the power that can be brought to bear. It is analogous to planning a seed. Even if properly cared for, it simply might not grow. As odd as it may seem for a book on sorcery to suggest, realistic expectations are called for. If a working fails, analyse the actual outcome and attempt to gain new insights on why it differs from that which is desired. Then try again, applying this new insight.

I proffer that the concept of the magical link is informational in nature, and that it can be explained by several of the principles which describe the interaction via wave physics of multiple vibrating systems. The most applicable of these are *resonance* and *entrainment*.

Resonance and Entrainment

Almost every physical system, whether mechanical, electromagnetic, biological, quantum, or thermodynamic in nature has an inherent frequency at which it will vibrate more efficiently than any other when oscillating energy is applied to it. Consequently, this is known as the system's resonant frequency. In addition, two or more systems can be in resonance with one another if they are vibrating at the same frequency or if one is vibrating at a harmonic frequency of the other. A harmonic frequency, or simply *harmonic* for short, is one which is an integer multiple, such as two, three, etc. of the resonant frequency.

Although a state of vibration can be induced at nearly any frequency in a given system, it is only at the resonant frequencies that the vibrations tend not to dissipate. Instead, the vibrations stabilize, and a standing wave gets formed. This occurs when points on the waveform, called *nodes*, appear to stand still as the existing vibrations in the system encounter interference with further incoming vibrations at the resonant frequency or one of its harmonic frequencies.

This phenomenon could provide a reason why magic does not always work to the degree which is desired. Since the resonant frequencies of structures in underlying fundamental matter are not known, there is no way to guarantee resonance will occur between projected intent and these structures. Fortunately, a form of resonance can be established even between systems of differing frequencies through one form of the process of entrainment.

In 1665, Christian Huygens discovered that two pendulum clocks in close proximity to each other whose pendulums were swinging at different rates would adjust over a period of time until they were in synchronization. If he intervened and disturbed the rate of one of the pendulums, it would again return to the same frequency, as long as it was near the other clock. Upon further observation he determined that the vibrations from the pendulums were being transmitted through the beam on which both clocks were hanging. When he moved the clocks apart, the effect would diminish, and the clocks would eventually fall out of synch. This form of synchronization is variously known as entrainment, phase locking, or frequency pulling.

The case that Huygens observed is an example of *spontaneous entrainment*. This effect occurs when the resonant frequencies of two or more vibrational systems are very similar. When this happens, the system vibrating at a faster rate loses energy, some transfers to the slower vibrating system, and some dissipates into the environment.

There is also another form of this phenomenon, known as *forced* or *driven entrainment*. This occurs when one system exerts influence over another and forces it to vibrate at a frequency which may or may not be natural for it. This happens either through a massive application of force, or a persistently applied lower degree of force over time (Collier and Burch, 2000). Depending on the fragility of the system which is the recipient of this effect, it may get damaged or destroyed in the process. An example of this is when a crystal wine glass is shattered by the application of high frequency sound waves.

In either type of entrainment, information is transferred between the participating systems. In the case of forced entrainment, pre-existing information passes to the system being subsumed. In spontaneous entrainment, a new information state is created which is less complex the closer the participating systems get to synchronization. This decrease in complexity is due to the lesser amount of information required to describe the newly combined relationship between systems.

Forced entrainment, particularly when it can cause resonance, and thus a self-reinforcing pattern in another system, has immense potential for imparting information. This is the goal of sorcery, to formulate a desire, encode it somehow into a message in a form of information that can be effectively transmitted, and then sending that message forth. The question of whether human consciousness can influence external systems directly has also been a subject of study by physicists.

Anomalies Research

In 1979, Princeton physicist Robert Jahn established PEAR, the Princeton Engineering Anomalies Research program. The purpose of this project was "to pursue rigorous scientific study of the interaction of human consciousness with sensitive physical devices, systems, and processes common to contemporary engineering practice" (PEAR, 2005). One of the primary activities of the program was to study anomalies which occur in interactions between machines which generate random events, and human operators who attempt to influence the outcomes in a specified way.

Over the first 12 years of the program, 91 anonymous operators performed over 2.4 million trials with an electronic random event generator, or REG. An analysis of the composite results database for these trials indicates that although the influence exerted at the individual level is small, that a strong overall relationship exists between operator intent and an actual achieved influence. The probability of achieving the composite results of the study is approximately 3.5×10^{-13}, which is less than one in one trillion.

The machine anomaly investigations are framed within the context of *psychokinesis*, or PK, the theorized human ability to manipulate matter and motion through the power of the mind. It is my contention that the differences between what are typically referred to as psychic abilities and sorcery are purely semantic. Both disciplines involve the manipulation or non-local perception of phenomenal reality through the exertion of Will and mental intent by a human being. It is true that many forms of magical practice attribute the ultimate source of their power to sources external to the self, but the success of the PEAR trials illustrate in an analytical and reproducible way that such belief is not essential for the desired results to be achieved.

By further example, some of the parallels between the methods used by the PEAR operators and those proposed in the system of sorcery created by Austin Osman Spare are remarkable. As I described in chapter one, Spare considered it essential that the sorcerer achieve a state of vacuity of mind which he referred to as "Neither-Neither" in order to prevent the psychic censor from inhibiting the success of a magical operation. Likewise, in attempting to influence random events, Jahn and co-author Brenda Dunne found that operators who were in a state of relaxation or mild hypnosis induced by sound or visual stimuli, and thus prevented from actively focusing on their task were actually more effective in manifesting an influence. They refer to this beneficially distracted mental state as the "space between the bits," or the "world between the worlds" (Jahn and Dunne, 2001).

The conclusion reached, as a result of the PEAR trials, is that rather than the conscious mind directly manipulating tangible matter (as was first believed) it appears to be the unconscious mind which manipulates reality at a sub-tangible level. A model was conceived in which the conscious mind passes its intent to the unconscious (in much the same way that Spare's sigils do), which then engages reality at the intangible level indicated by such (now hopefully recognizable) terms as the implicate order, strings or quantum foam. These interactions are propagated upward through the quantum particulate level and ultimately to the tangible and perceivable level of physical matter.

The model of reality proposed by Jahn and other PEAR researchers has been criticized by some as being only a metaphor, and not reflecting actual physical interactions between the mind and matter. In response to such criticism, Jahn and Dunne (1997) replied:

> *This troubles us little, for upon deeper reflection, all of science is, to a large degree, metaphoric... metaphor is not a sloppy form of conceptual representation; it is a critical step in establishing the foundations of any objective science, and it will be even more indispensable in creating a subjective* science.

The conclusion reached by Jahn and Dunne is that the interface between the unconscious and the intangible implies an as of yet still unknown process which actually performs the action of influence. They theorized that at this deepest level of existence, referred to by Jahn as *subliminal seed space*, that the division between mental and physical phenomena breaks down, in effect creating a continuum of information which flows freely between mind and matter (Jahn and Dunne, 2001). Reports from some of the most successful operators who have taken part in the trials revealed that they experienced a bonding with the machine, as if they merged with it into a single system (Jahn and Dunne, 1997). Some operators also referred to this effect as *resonance*.

Far from being a mere metaphor, resonance may be the actual process by which influence over the machine is exerted. This possibility becomes more interesting when considered in concert with other theories which examine the wave natures of both consciousness and physical reality itself.

The Holonomic Brain in the Implicate Order

Several of the underlying models of physical reality that I have discussed, such as Bohm's Implicate Order, and string theory are particularly sensitive to the concept of resonance, as they are based on waveforms at their most fundamental level. In the former case, the holomovement acts as a carrier wave which transmits the implicate order until such time as the information enfolded within it is explicated, creating the illusion of matter and motion. In the latter case, the vibrational rate of the individual strings dictates which fundamental particle a particular string will manifest as at the tangible scale.

In order to better understand the nature of reality, David Bohm notes that, the origin of the word reality itself comes from the Latin *res*, which means "thing." *Res* in turn is derived from the verb *reri*, which means "to think," which implies that a thing is that which is thought about. Within the framework of the implicate order, the belief that the thing and the thought are separate must be abandoned, as each is only part of the same process, and have relevance only regarding each other. Unfortunately, Bohm speculated that since the implicate order itself is beyond the reach of human knowledge, the ultimate nature of the relationship between thing and thought cannot be described (Bohm, 1980).

Karl Pribram's holonomic brain theory attempts to explain the link that Bohm could not fathom. As I introduced in chapter seven, Pribram's theory, like Bohm's, was based on the model of a hologram, but at the micro scale of human consciousness as opposed to the macro scale of the universe. Bohm posed the question of whether or not the actual nature and cause of conscious could be understood, if it is accepted that the implicate order is its underlying process. He cites Pribram's research as the key to the understanding that consciousness and matter are part of the same system. This conclusion is a natural one, and is already implied by the fact that consciousness as a process is a subset of everything else that exists in the universe, and therefore would have developed subject to the laws which govern the larger whole.

Although the fusion of Pribram and Bohm's ideas provides a model which explains how the brain interprets the unfolding of the implicate order into the explicate order via its own holographic processes, this combined theory makes the assumption that the purpose of consciousness is only to translate the incoming information carried by the holomovement. There is a form of reciprocity and feedback in the process, but it is limited largely to the form of memory, which is characterized as a lower-resolution playback of experienced reality. No explicit mechanism is proposed for projecting desires from the consciousness back into the implicate order for the purpose of influencing it, although there is the kernel of such an idea in Bohm's theory if it is viewed in a particular way.

If there is an infinite number of super- and sub- implicate orders as Bohm suggests, and higher orders organize lower orders, and are in turn influenced by these lower orders, then what is the result of considering the conscious mind as a discrete sub-implicate order? If Pribram's theory is correct, then the methods through which the brain encodes and decodes consciousness and memory are directly analogous to the behaviour of the implicate order itself. Given this scenario, and the observation that the brain as a system is an embedded subsystem of the larger universe, the argument can be made that consciousness does have a mechanism to provide input into the behaviour of processes larger than itself.

If the brain as "hardware" and the mind as "software" have the capability to receive and decode raw information from the environment, then I propose that it is through the reverse of this process, employing the principles of entrainment and resonance that influence over the environment is achieved. I further suggest that this is the physical mechanism by which the results generated in the PEAR trials were achieved. This satisfies Jahn's belief in the continuum of information through a set of physical principles such as those that are well understood at the macro scale. As such, based on models developed as part of string theory, these same processes are believed to describe the physics of waves down to the smallest perceivable scale.

Summary

The concept of the magical link between a real-world entity and a symbolic representation of it is a well-known component of sympathetic magic and sorcery. This is part of a broader set of principles, the laws of similarity and contagion. I propose that the magical link is actually informational in nature, and that it can be understood in terms of wave physics.

Nearly every physical system has an inherent resonant frequency at which it tends to vibrate if energy is applied to it. Integer multiples of this frequency, called harmonics, can have a similar effect on it. If multiple systems have similar or harmonic resonant frequencies, then they can more easily exchange information while minimizing energy loss to the environment.

The principles of entrainment and resonance describe the process by which two vibrating or oscillating systems with similar or harmonic resonant frequencies can enter a state of synchronized vibration, or spontaneous entrainment, and by which one system can induce its frequency on another, by means of forced entrainment.

Studies at Jahn's PEAR program assembled a body of trials which suggest that humans can influence the result of electronic random number generators through the exertion of Will alone. Further studies indicated that this is likely a subconscious process which takes place at the smallest scale of reality. At this level of existence, smaller than the fundamental particles which constitute matter, thought and physicality intermingle in an exchange of information and potential. It is my position that this research provides statistical validation that human consciousness does have the capability to influence physical reality, and that this is in fact the causal force behind sorcery.

The consideration of David Bohm's theory of the implicate order in combination with Karl Pribram's holonomic model of the brain suggests that the brain decodes stimuli from its environment by a method which is strongly anomalous to holography. The conscious mind, conceived as a microcosmic model of the universe itself, is therefore a form of sub-implicate order. Through the infinite scale of nested orders, it could have an effect on the enfolded state of the larger universe, which could then influence the universe as manifest.

Connecting the concepts discussed in this and prior chapters leads to a model in which the subconscious mind acts as an agent of the conscious mind, by distilling its Will into a packet of information through which it can be propagated into physical reality at the most fundamental level of existence. At this scale, the smallest perturbation can have a profound effect on the behaviour of larger systems which form as the scale is propagated into the phenomenal universe. The next chapter investigates some of the physical mechanisms by which this transmission of Will might be accomplished.

Chapter 9
Influence and Information

Universe will respond non-locally to my thought. Maybe it will average out to a microscopic or invisible response most of the time, but occasionally things may wobble and jump visibly.

– Robert Anton Wilson

In chapter eight, I introduced a few possibilities that explain how human consciousness might be capable of influencing the behaviour of matter and energy, but some mechanism is still needed to actually act as a carrier of intent to make this happen. This chapter explores several possible methods available via human physiology which could fulfil this capacity. One debate that has arisen in physics circles is whether the universe can best be thought of in terms of atoms or bits, whether a physical model or an information model will ultimately lead to the best understanding of existence. From the standpoint of influencing experiential reality, either model is acceptable, but the latter may be more advantageous.

Communication theory (Shannon, 1948) provides a set of concepts that are at least analogous to, and possibly literally descriptive of, the process that must take place to send out intent. The brain acts as the information source, creating a message which is designed to be interpreted by the recipient, which in this case is comprised of the fundamental material of space-time at its smallest scale and the energetic and ephemeral structures which exist at that ultra-microscopic level. This message is transmitted in some way, the means of which I investigate, along a channel which is electromagnetic in nature. The message is received, and assuming that it has not been rendered incomprehensible by the noise inherent in the transmission process, as described in chapter two, it can be interpreted and acted on, causing the desired results.

In the previous chapter, I referred to a theoretical packet of information which the subconscious mind would use to encode Will and intent for transmission outward. This constitutes the message which is to be transmitted. It would likely be a far simpler unit of information than the memory engrams that Karl Lashely and subsequent brain researchers have been ultimately unable to locate. The information contained in such a packet would need to consist only of intent distilled down to its most primal and concentrated form. It must be assumed that the universe does not need literal instructions on how to bring about desired results, and in fact it has been my experience that an attempt to engage in such micro-management of incipient reality usually brings less favourable results than if the means to the end are left unspecified.

Although there has been speculation that the way in which the brain produces thought resembles a digital process, it is physically analogue in nature. Although individual neurons are analogous to logic gates in a digital circuit, the analogy is not perfect. The intensity of stimulus to which a neuron is subjected plays a role in whether or not it transmits or suppresses the impulse it receives (von Neumann, 1958). In addition, besides reacting only to internal impulses, neurons may also be activated by external stimuli such as light, sound, or pressure. The brain is both less precise in its ability to calculate, and more resilient in its ability to recover from signal failure than a digital system. In digital systems, the loss of only a single bit of information can cause an unrecoverable corruption or loss of meaning. In contrast, the lower level of precision and more granular method in which the brain functions serves to diminish the significance of the inadvertent omission or addition of information to a transmission. The brain possesses a quality often referred to as *neuroplasticity*. This refers to the capability of neurons to create new connections or even assume different functions if parts of the brain are damaged (Schwartz and Begley, 2002). It is likely due to this analogue nature that any particular discretely encoded unit of thought or memory has eluded discovery. If there is some sort of "thought quantum" which can carry information out of the brain, it too must be analogue in nature, at least while it is still internal to the human system.

Ultimately the exact nature of the interaction between the information emanated by the human body and the processes of the physical universe are not known with any actual certainty. Those researchers who have documented the occurrence of influence being exerted over external matter and energy by human subjects have produced theories, but no one has yet even devised a possible framework by which these theories could be tested to isolate an exact process.

Once intent has been successfully broadcast and received, there are several ways conceivable in which the underlying mechanics might function. Two possibilities which come immediately to mind are some type of entrainment imposed by directed human energy, and the possibility of an imbalance created at the quantum level via this interaction which survives the typical process in which the fluctuations tend to cancel each other out as scale increases into the perceivable.

In a sense, the most fundamental level of existence consists of noise from which information self-organizes. The universe emanates from this randomness and turbulence.

This is the potential, the chaos, from which order is constructed. Mythology holds that this action is the exclusive purview of gods, but from what has been theorized in several cosmological models, it is the nature of the material itself to generate existence through fluctuations without the need of external influence. A sorcerer has learned to apply direction to this process, and by doing so has acquired the potential to pull forth the desired result from the myriad possibilities.

Vital Energy

The concept of an energy field which encompasses or even emanates from all living organisms has been present for thousands of years in many different cultures. Some of these cultures differ on the perspective of causality, and whether life generates this energy, or conversely that life itself is only a physical manifestation of it. Regardless, one general similarity persists: that a universal energy or proto-energy is present in all of nature. Later cultures further developed this concept, as well as the idea that through discipline and openness to its subtle nature, mankind can learn to focus it to desired ends.

The Indo-Europeans, due to their widespread migrations, had a profound social and linguistic effect on Europe, and western Asia. A modern reconstruction of the proposed Proto-Indo-European language, which is done by comparing word roots from descendent languages, has revealed some details of the cosmology of this cultural group. One of these is the concept of *aiw, which has been identified as the PIE word root meaning "vital force." This concept can be found in several languages and religions which inherited it.

In Greece, *aiw was the source of several word and

concepts, including *aion*, which meant a long period of time (hence long life), and *pneuma*, the combination of the elements of air and fire which was envisioned by members of the Stoic school of philosophy as being the motivating principle responsible for action, thought, and motion. **Aiw* appears in the 3,000-year-old Hindu *Upanishad* scriptures as *prana*, which is a vital life energy which can manifest as breath in the material realm. It is a motivational force which drives action and is also believed to be present in sexual fluids and blood. Through the practice of yoga, control over the movement of prana throughout the body is believed to be possible for the purpose of increasing personal vitality.

Later, in the multipartite ancient Germanic conception of the soul, the breath of life was the *Athem* (Thorsson, 1989). It feeds and sustains the self and binds the body and soul together. It is thought to be the Breath of Odin, given to all living things at birth (Blumetti, 2010). Although this term has its origin in a different Proto-Indo-European root word for breath, the parallels show the intertwined nature of the breath and the energetic force in both the physical and subtle bodies.

Not all concepts of vital energy can be traced back to Indo-European roots. The civilization which independently emerged in modern-day China also included the concept under the name of *qi* (chi) or breath. Written records over 3,000 years old describe the practice of *qi gong*, or breath work, through which the movement and focus of qi is achieved. Qi is a central concept in many martial arts and meditational practices which are still practiced in the 21st century. Entire bodies of work have been dedicated to mastering these techniques, and I encourage research beyond the scope of this brief mention.

Although a vital energy paradigm is not as prominent in later European belief systems as in the east, the concept was not entirely abandoned. In the 17th century, an awareness of vital energy was incorporated into the philosophy of *Vitalism* whose adherents believed that mechanical processes were inadequate to explain life, and that a vital energy must also be present to explain it. The foundation of Vitalism was a classification scheme in which organic and inorganic matter were believed to be fundamentally different. This philosophy dropped in popularity as advances in chemistry in the early 19th century led to the discrediting of the classification scheme upon which it was based.

In the 20th century, vital force re-appeared in another form as *orgone* energy in a theory developed in the late 1930s by psychoanalyst Wilhelm Reich. In orgone theory, the supposed energy released at orgasm is thought to be connected to a larger force present in all life. Reich's theory received a great deal of criticism from his peers, and this combined with a federal investigation due to his past political affiliations resulted in a ban on orgone therapy, the destruction of his research, and his eventual imprisonment. Despite these circumstances, his work still has a small but ardent following.

The vital energy model is less couched in the western scientific paradigm than others, but this alone does not render it any less valid in terms of its ability to produce results. Individuals who wish to acknowledge the interconnectedness of life forms which this system implies might find it useful, as might those who choose to include a spiritual aspect in their sorcery, such as the belief in persistent external god forms.

One notable example of a modern magical system that

employs this model is that of Neo-Hermeticist Franz Bardon. He detailed the practice of using the entire skin surface as an organ to gather vital power from the *Akasa*, or etheric principle, and convey it to the body (Bardon, 1956). He suggested that this *Pore Breathing* could also be used along with visualisation to concentrate power within any desired part of the body. This accumulated energy can then be used for the loading of talismans, curing the sick, or any other purpose the magician wishes.

Biophotons

In the early 20th century, attempts by researchers to better understand the concept of a biological energy field led to the discovery that a measurable field is produced by almost all living cells. In 1922, Russian biologist Alexander Gurvich discovered through studies performed on plants that biological cells emit a very weak form of radiation which he believed had a positive influence on the rate of cellular division and growth. He named his discovery *mitogenic rays*. By experimenting on which materials were capable of filtering out or shielding against the transmission of these rays, Gurvich deduced that they likely fall within the ultraviolet portion of the electromagnetic spectrum.

Subsequent to Gurvich's discovery, little work was done in further investigating the nature of the rays until after World War II, and much of this was done under the assumption that they were essentially a metabolic waste product of electrochemical processes in the cell rather than a catalytic force. It was not until 1974 when Fritz-Albert Popp began studying the phenomenon with more sensitive instruments that more of their characteristics became known. In 1996 Popp founded the International Institute of Biophysics in Germany to focus on biological energy research.

Over a course of studies, Popp discovered that the rays, which have come to be known as *biophotons*, are actually not purely ultraviolet in nature, but that they are emitted fairly evenly across the infrared and visual portions of the spectrum as well (Popp, 1999). It is only the low absolute intensity in terms of the number of photons emitted, from a low of only a few photons per cell per day up to a maximum of approximately one hundred photons per second per square centimetre of surface area, which prevents the human eye from being able to detect this radiation directly.

Another attribute that Popp observed is that biophotons are coherent except in cases of biological anomaly. For example, the wavelengths of photons emitted from healthy cells tend to be in phase with one another, but those emitted from cancerous cells are disordered in nature. It is this coherence that caused Popp to theorize that this emission of radiation is not some sort of waste process, but rather a fundamental component of cellular development and inter-cellular communication within a biological system. As coherent light has a greater capacity for transmitting information with less loss than light that is not in phase does, this discovery was particularly important to the latter theory. Ultimately, Popp concluded that metabolic activity in biological systems is actually governed by the biophoton field. He theorized that this is established via a permanent feedback coupling between the field and living matter in which the field dictates the distribution of the matter, and the matter in turn provides the boundary conditions of the field (Popp, 2006). This portion of Popp's theory has yet to be disproved, but it is not widely held among other researchers in the field.

Biophotons carry information not only between cells in an organism, but also outside of the organism into the surrounding environment. However in order to utilize this effect for any directed purpose such as carrying intent, there must be some method of controlling their behaviour. The ability of individuals to modulate their own photonic and electromagnetic output has been the focus of several research studies which have investigated the effect as it pertains to bioenergy healing.

A pilot study conducted by a team led by William Joines (2004), of Duke University and the Rhine Research Centre recorded increased light emission as well as the change in electrical charge on the skin of one of their subjects (Tiller, 2004). As an example of the quantification that is possible in such research, Joines cites a study led by biofeedback pioneer Elmer Green which measured only electrical charge, reporting a median change of 8.3 volts of bioelectric potential among study participants who were attempting to alter their own field strengths. In 2017, a series of studies on biophotonic emission by touch healers showed that intent affected the number of photons emitted from the hands of practitioners, with bursts occurring at during the time period of greatest exertion (Rubik and Jabs, 2017).

Other research on human influence over external phenomena has resulted in the postulation of fundamental forces and states besides those in the Standard Model. William Tiller, professor emeritus of material sciences at Stanford University has investigated the effects of directed human intent in a number of experiments. By way of *Intention Imprinted Electrical Devices*, which are electronic oscillators which have been imprinted with statements of intent by experienced meditators, Tiller has found that factors such as the pH of purified water, thermodynamic activity in enzymes, and the development speed of fruit fly larvae can be influenced (Tiller, 2004).

Based on the results of numerous experiments, Tiller hypothesizes that physical reality consists of two separate levels which demonstrate a variable degree of coupling. The more familiar reality of known particles and forces is thought to co-exist with a previously undetected vacuum state which is subject to manipulation via direct action from human consciousness.

The results of these types of studies are often criticized as falling into the realm of pseudo-science, even those which are deemed to have been conducted in a rigorous fashion which would otherwise satisfy the criteria for experiments in more established fields. Those authorities who are quick to condemn or ridicule this type of research must not forget that now widely accepted theories such as gravity, quantum theory, and biophoton emission itself were similarly treated during their developmental years.

Scepticism is a useful tool for critical analysis, but it sometimes leads to its own form of dogma, in which ideas which do not fit into the personal worldview of the review are rejected without consideration. It is true that not all positive results which are reported can be duplicated by other investigators, but it is also true that not all who attempt to perform conformational studies do so without a pre-conceived negative bias against their subject matter.

Sorcery is not constrained to adhere to the scientific method, and complete reproducibility of results is not a criterion in selecting which techniques to use. A sceptic would most likely dismiss the successful results of a magical operation as a coincidence. Conversely, a sorcerer might consider the inability to accept an ongoing series of fortuitous coincidences as something deeper to be indicative of wilful inflexibility of perception. In such a case, the differences in the subjective realities in which the conflicting points of view are grounded are not likely to be resolved within the current socio-scientific framework.

From a Quantum Sorcery standpoint, the biophoton model draws on the discovery by Arthur Compton in 1922 that a photon was capable of transferring energy to, and thus altering the momentum of, a particle such as an electron. Photons emitted by the body interact with individual particles in the environment. This in turn initiates a series of events at the subatomic scale which cascade upward in scale into the perceivable, physical world. This method is possibly the crudest in terms of its brute force approach to transmitting information, but in its projectile nature, it is also likely the easiest to visualise for many users.

Direct Non-Local Interaction

The final model for projecting intent that I examine is the possibility of a direct, non-local interface between human consciousness and reality at the most fundamental level. This model utilizes the principle of quantum entanglement and builds upon concepts introduced by Jahn and Dunne in their Modular Model of Mind/Matter Manifestations (Jahn and Dunne, 2001).

One of the arguments for a mechanism of influence which is not directly related to a typical macro-scale electromagnetic field is that information exchange in the anomalies recorded in the PEAR trials are independent of distance, physical shielding, and time (Nelson, 1999). The first two variables become limiting factors on the intensity of such a field, diminishing if not eliminating its capability to exert an influence. This alone would not disqualify a classical energy-based explanation, but when operators in the trials were apparently able to exert an influence on an event in the future, or more incredibly in the past, then classical field models are no longer adequate to explain this capability.

In this model, the division between the self and the rest of the universe is thought to be an illusory construct of the human ego. As such, information is understood to move freely and bi-directionally between a sorcerer and the surrounding world, as it is only the ego which persists in creating the division between the two. Once the ego is conditioned to relax, this division will erode, and a connection with the greater whole can be established. This process is similar in some ways to a shamanic initiation, and at an advanced level, the end result would likely be similar to the state of *alternity* described by John Lilly in which all possible paths in space-time are opened up to the sorcerer.

If the consciousness of an individual is considered as a local, coherent region within the larger universe rather than as a discrete entity, then applying the principle of quantum entanglement and the associated property of instantaneous communication of information satisfies the apparent requirements for transmitting intent. As the states of photons within the coherent field generated by the brain are altered by the encoding of information and intent, their entangled counterparts outside of this field are correspondingly altered as well. This provides the impetus to start the scale-escalating cascade which I described previously.

Similarly, I propose that within this model the coherence of the localized field of consciousness within the brain prevents a reverse process from taking place. The quantum states of photons within our brains are shielded from random influence which might otherwise occur as the entangled external particles are subjected to forces in their locality. The individual drive of the self to be separate from that which is not the self transcends the division between consciousness and sub-conscious thought processes. It acts to reinforce this local coherence even as it insinuates the heretical notion that "mere" human beings are capable of altering external reality by Will alone.

The validity of applying non-local quantum scale effects to events at the macro-scale of physical existence is still being debated. The implication that information can travel faster than the speed of light, even if energy cannot, leads also to the suggestion that the information is already present in all places, and is not actually traveling at all. As it happens, this is exactly what David Bohm states in his implicate order theory. The possibility of super-luminal information transfer has been interpreted by some believers as supportive evidence which could explain telepathy and possibly other anomalous effects. This argument still faces stiff resistance among sceptics.

Summary

Each of the models I have examined has been suggested at some point or another as the mechanism by which anomalous events can be made to occur by manifesting human intent. Not all who study these effects would consider them to be sorcery, but from a functional standpoint, the label is appropriate. This mechanism is largely independent of both the belief structure surrounding the practitioner, as well as the exact methods used to reach a physical state which is conducive to projecting the Will.

Communication theory offers a set of concepts which may be useful to envision and describe the way in which intent is encoded by the sorcerer for projection into external reality. Within this scenario, the brain formulates a message which consists of symbols to be interpreted by the processes which operate to create reality at the smallest scale of existence.

The concept of a vital energy field which surrounds all life forms dates to the earliest civilizations. It has survived for thousands of years in the forms of various martial arts and philosophical systems, and still has adherents who embrace the concept of being connected to a larger source of energy and life.

The desire to better understand this proposed biological energy field led to the experimental discovery of mitogenic rays, now known as biophotons, by Alexander Gurvich. Subsequent research by Fritz-Albert Popp led to the discovery that measurable, coherent energy is emitted by most living cells, although the mechanism behind the production of this energy is disputed by factions which variously consider it to be an organizational force which provides a template for matter to manifest, or merely a metabolic by-product of normal cellular processes. Bioenergy studies which analyse the effect of healing intent projected over a distance, as well as the measurable changes which occur in the physiology of the healer are cited as examples of this model in action.

The results achieved in the PEAR trials in which humans have shown a statistically significant capability to exert influence over external random systems are studied as an example, as these results cannot be explained by normal energy field actions alone. With this in mind, I propose that quantum entanglement and non-local action is a likely explanation for the mechanism behind the projection of intent. Within this model, consciousness is envisioned as a coherent local field which maintains one-way control over entangled photons, simultaneously providing a conduit for exerting Will and preventing the manipulation of internal quantum states by external forces acting on entangled constituent photons.

These models are all offered as possibilities. There is no experimental basis for designating any one as being more or less likely than another for providing the connection between the microcosm of the self, and the macrocosm of the larger universe. The actual mechanism may in fact be none of these, but each is suitable for incorporating into a personal system of sorcery.

Chapter 10
Visualisation and Will

Reality is up for grabs, so learn the codes through which the narrative is crafted and participate in its unfolding

– Douglas Rushkoff

This chapter addresses the creation of a personal system of sorcery using principles of quantum mechanics, wave physics, and chaos theory. As with any type of magical practice, the effectiveness of these techniques depends on the belief and Will of the person using them. In using the information presented here, the degree to which you personally believe that these specific principles are the mechanism by which magic is accomplished is far less important than the belief that phenomenal reality, if there truly is such a thing, can be altered by the projection of Will.

Throughout this book, I have endeavoured to present material which is intended to create awareness that as observers of the physical processes of the universe that we are also active participants in its ongoing creation. Even as I have taken this approach, I realise that not everyone believes that it is a good idea to look for an explanation of the physical forces behind the effect that we call magic. Some might condemn such an investigation as materialist short-sightedness, the metaphysical misuse of science, or the wrongful exclusion of ascendant external entities to which they attribute these forces. At various points in my study and practice of magic, I might have counted myself among each of those camps, but in this speculative field, there is no right or wrong approach; there are only systems which produce desired results for their users, and those which do not. In this system I have found plausible

Dave Smith

explanations to satisfy my desire to understand the process, as well as methods of using these principles to yield the results I desire.

Metaphor and Visualisation

A great deal of this chapter consists of metaphorical language which describes a basic system of focusing and projecting the Will. Although I do not believe that the mechanisms which sorcery is based upon have inherent sensory actions associated with them, I do believe that it is easier to grasp concepts which are framed in this way than it is to use a system based on purely abstract information which cannot be addressed by sensory cues.

I have mentioned the technique of visualisation several times in prior chapters. Visualisation is simply the creation of an internal mental image, whether for an event or an object which has literally been seen, and then "replayed" via memory, or for a scene or object which exists only in the mind, and has no corresponding physical reality. Although by strict definition, the term refers only to the simulation of visual imagery, the process need not be limited to this, and can include other sensations as well.

Another word frequently used interchangeably with visualisation is imagination. Stop for a moment and consider this word. Unfortunately, "imagination" is often used as a dismissive or pejorative term to suggest that a person is perceiving reality inaccurately, based on the assumptions on reality held by others. The ability to create detailed visual imagery with the mind's eye is an important process in sorcery. The greater the accuracy with which a desired scenario can be constructed, the lesser the amount of intent and energy required to manifest that scenario into reality.

Learning to visualise is not terribly difficult but it requires a great deal of practice to develop a suitable degree of focus and control for it to be useful for magical purposes. While visualisation used in ritual or active magical work may often be done while standing, I have found that for practice and development, a quiet, comfortable place to sit or recline while doing so is beneficial. A good place to start with for practice is by remembering a favourite childhood toy, or other object of personal meaning. With your eyes closed, picture the object in your mind as if you were seeing it with open eyes. Start with a broad overall view of the object. Rotate the view of the item and visualise it from all possible angles. Work on this process until a complete image of the object is formed in your mind. Once the basic process is mastered, begin to visualise other objects, places, or people that are familiar. As this too becomes easier over time, move on to items which you have never actually seen.

Knowing when this skill has been adequately developed is an individual judgment. There is no absolute measure of success or failure in terms of the degree of accuracy which is required for the successful use of visualisation in magic. Only the analysis of whether attempted magical operations are successfully meeting the expectations of their creator can be used to determine whether more practice is needed in crafting the microcosmic model of desired reality.

Another visual exercise I recommend is the creation of the ideal self. "Ideal" in this regard means only "as you Will it to be". Picture yourself in your mind as you would ideally wish yourself to be in both a physical and mental sense. This image may be vastly different from your actual form. This is completely acceptable, but the closer the ideal self is to a form which is an achievable possibility, the more likely it will be that your actual self can be shaped to conform to your ideal.

Each time this form is pictured, the process reinforces your subconscious mind that this is how you should rightly appear. Eventually, if a degree of physical effort is incorporated as well, the body can become closer to the personal ideal. In addition, this exercise serves to create an avatar of the self which can use in third-person perspective visualised scenarios.

The Personal Energy Field

Once a personally acceptable level of proficiency at visualisation is achieved, the next exercise is to develop an awareness of, and control over, the personal energy field. This is a hybrid construct that is partially literal, and partially virtual. It consists of both the physical coherent electromagnetic energy field which surrounds the body, and a visualisation of the potential for projecting and focusing intent to do magical work, as was discussed in chapter two. Learning to focus and project this construct is essential for performing many of the techniques to follow. This field is not exactly the same as the etheric body or aura of Theosophy or the yogic *kosa*, but there are some similarities with both of these representations. The intensity of the physical aspect of the personal field diminishes over distance from the body, but there are no distinct layers corresponding to different aspects of the spirit in this model.

In addition to the actual output of bioenergy from the body, the personal field can be strengthened through visualisation exercises. This is done by envisioning energy materializing out of the air around the field much like water vapor condenses into liquid. As this energy is drawn in, it increases the intensity of the existing field as it is assimilated and entrained into coherency. This process may also cause a feeling of warmth on the skin, and an increased feeling of vitality. Use this technique prior to performing many of the exercises listed in this chapter.

This technique can also be used to take in negative energy from an environment and convert it to a neutral or positive intent. From this point, it can either be kept, or released back into the world. This is similar to the Tibetan Buddhist practice of *Tonglen*, in which the practitioner breathes in suffering, and breathes out joy and comfort.

There are also times where you may want to discharge excess energy from the personal field without performing a magical operation. This can be accomplished by visualising energy radiating outward from the core of the body. Inhale long and slow, hold the breath for a moment, then exhale, visualising a spherical wave of energy expanding outward from the core of the body behind the navel. This wave pushes outward in all directions, expanding and increasing in diameter until the energy invested in it has been dissipated. This can be an effective way to disperse excess energy prior to meditation or sleep.

In visualising bioenergy, the colour of the energy is more a function of the beliefs and personal associations of the sorcerer than of any physical attribute or codified system. Although the first examples identified by Gurvich fell in the ultraviolet portion of the spectrum, Popp's later research showed that the energy is emitted in the infrared and visible portions of the spectrum as well. Traditionally in several magical systems, certain colours are associated with specific effects, but this has always been more a matter of human psychology than of any hard and fast rule. I suggest the use of whichever associations work best for the individual sorcerer. In the following examples, I will describe the colours that I use in my own visualisations.

Basic Magical Operations

While I am sure that many readers already have their own preferred set of magical exercises that are far more comprehensive and intricate than the ones presented below, I nevertheless want to provide a set of basic suggestions to serve as a foundation for those who do not. The visualisation of intent is very largely subjective and personal to each sorcerer who practices it. The exercises in this chapter are based on my own techniques and are intended primarily to serve as examples for the construction of various types of magical operations. It is my assertion that no pre-written ritual or spell will ever be as effective as one which is created by the person who will be using it.

Incidentally, the reason that I use the generic term "operation" more frequently than the more common "spell" is largely a matter of semantics. From a linguistic standpoint a spell is a spoken incantation, whereas the generic term encompasses a wider array of spoken, written, physical, and mental components.

Shielding

The creation of a personal shield or barrier against unwanted influence or energy is one of the first and most useful operations that a sorcerer can learn. The basic principle is to extend and intensify the personal energy field to a desired distance around the self. There is by default no specific size or shape that this shield should take. Some prefer that the shape of this space mimics their physical body at some distance; others may visualise it as an egg or sphere. This projection usually fills a space equivalent to the personal zone of interaction, or "personal space", which ranges from one to four feet away from the body. This construct is analogous to a suit of armour, or the energy shields that are ubiquitous in works of science fiction, as opposed to the definition of a larger autonomous space that will be discussed further in the chapter.

Some sorcerers may be tempted to render their shields as impenetrable barriers. I disagree with this practice, as it tends to diminish the ability to receive sensory input. Instead I advocate visualising a field of increasing density and resistance, so that the outer edge acts a "ward off" zone, and only at the closest point to the body does the barrier become largely impermeable. In this way, it not only functions as a protective barrier, but as an extension of sensory awareness rather than as an inhibitor. In its most fundamental function, the shield acts as a transitional zone, separating and distinguishing the self from the "not-self" of the surrounding environment.

An alternate technique to shielding is to take in and assimilate incoming energy via forced entrainment rather than blocking it out. This is similar to the visualisation of increasing the personal field that was mentioned previously, but with a more forceful emphasis on entraining the newly acquired energy to match the personal field.

The actual visualisation for creating the shield can be performed from either a first- or third-person point of view. In either case, envision the energy field which projects from all parts of the body changing shape and intensity until it resembles the desired form. As this happens, the colour of the outer boundary of the shield will take on a white or silver appearance, with the increased albedo indicating the tendency to reflect unwanted energy.

Besides this encompassing technique, a more immediate and active shield may be accomplished through the assignment of a sharp vocalization, such as *Skjold!* (Old Norse) or *Scutum!* (Latin) with a "halt" or sweeping hand gesture, along with a projection of force in the direction of the threat.

Sensing

The development of a greater awareness of the self, and the way in which the self interacts with the surrounding environment is the focus of this operation. There are several exercises through which this faculty can be improved. The first of these techniques is to develop a personal sphere of awareness by learning the normal extent of physical perception, and then working to increase this distance.

To demonstrate this, close your eyes and hold your open hands in front of you facing each other at a distance of about eight inches. Begin to move them slowly together while concentrating on the sensation that is generated in the palms. At some point as they move closer together, a sensation of greater warmth may be felt. This may also be accompanied by a slight tingling feeling. If the sensation is not felt, try the visualisation to increase the personal field, and try again. When the sensation is felt, begin to slowly pull your hands apart. The warmth may persist for a greater distance pulling away than it did initially. The goal is to increase the distance at which the initial sensation can be first noticed.

When this process is successful, begin to try to sense other objects before they are touched. This is a talent that is developed and expanded over time and can lead to a greater degree of general awareness of both the body and the environment. This can be a boon in any number of situations.

One novel way to experience the effect of sensory enhancement is to move slowly through a darkened room, and to be aware the objects in the room. This should obviously be practiced with care to avoid injury, and I recommend you practice this activity in a familiar area before attempting to navigate through a completely unknown space. More than just a metaphysical practice, this exercise actually involves the sharpening of the human sense of *proprioception*, our awareness of our own body within space.

There is a meditation technique that I have found to be most useful for the expansion of awareness. From a comfortable seated position, sit with your eyes closed, and simply "breathe and be", focusing on your breath and reaching a relaxed state. Visualise yourself sitting in your space. Expand your focus to the entirety of the room. Next, zoom your perspective out until it encompasses the building. Continue in this manner, pulling your awareness further out. See the city, the nation, continent, planet, etc. around you. Spend some time at each level, trying to add as much detail as you can. When you have gone as far out as you wish, pull your focus back into yourself.

This practice is useful for developing and improving the skill of *remote perception*. This is typically considered a "psychic" ability rather than a magical one, but the distinction between "psi" disciplines and sorcery is ultimately only semantic, as both are accomplished through the exertion of energy and Will. Remote perception is the ability to passively visualise distant locations or events. One method of doing this is to focus on a known individual and then attempt to receive information about their surroundings and circumstances. This technique can be practiced by pre-arranging times at which attempts to perceive the other are made with a friend, and then contacting them later to determine how accurate the information received was. Another variant is for one person to draw some simple figure and then attempt to transmit the image to the perceiver, who will draw what they receive. Growing up in a Psi-friendly household, this was an exercise that my parents and I regularly engaged in when I was a teenager.

The increase in sensitivity that can result from these types of practices can also lead to a greater degree of proficiency in divination through other means, such as tarot or runes. The ability to better sense and interpret the subtle energies of the Universe is vital to this most foundational aspect of sorcery. We are constantly bathed in innumerable different fields of energy, and hence information. Another effect of increasing sensitivity is the ability to better perceive energy imprints in an area, or even those signatures of ostensibly non-corporeal entities, to whatever extent you believe in such. Obviously, if you have an established pattern of non-belief, improving this skill will not alter your capabilities in this regard.

Healing

As illustrated by the studies performed by the PEAR group and others, healing via visualisation is one of the most widely known uses of bioenergy. This exercise can be done either through physical touch, or remotely. For direct contact, place both hands on the body part most associated with the illness or injury. With eyes closed visualise cool blue energy flowing from your hands into the injured or ill tissues, revitalizing and invigorating them. Alternately, project a sense of well-being and optimal function into the body of your subject. Rely on the cells and systems of the body to know their functions and operate on the assumption that all systems will aspire to function in an optimal manner if given the opportunity to do so. This is a greatly simplified form of this operation. There are myriad systems of profound depth which focus on touch healing should you be interested in pursuing this discipline.

For healing at a distance, keep a photograph of the individual being healed, or some physical item of theirs to use in creating a magical link to the person. If no assisting item is available, remote healing can still be accomplished by visualising the recipient, but a greater degree of energy loss occurs during the process. In either case, visualise your energy traveling to the recipient and bathing the injured area of their body in the same cool, blue energy as before. If the specific area of the body is not known, simply use your energy to bolster their own energy field, so that their own processes can work on their injury more effectively.

This process can also be performed as a collaborative effort between multiple workers of Will. They need not even be practicing the same form of magic. The process can be further assisted by the distribution of the same image or symbol under which the working is to be performed to all participants. This is a perfect scenario in which to use the laws of similarity and contagion to increase the efficiency of the operation, and to maximize the yield from the energy expended.

Banishing

Banishing is used for several purposes, from preparing an area for magical work to driving away disturbing entities. A simple banishing can be done using no tools through a cycle of three energy-building breaths, with each inhalation slightly deeper than the last, followed each time by a gentle, non-projective exhalation. On the third breath, inhale as deeply as possible. On the exhale, push a spherical energy wave rapidly outward with a shout, or a short, easily articulated phrase. I call this technique a *flash banishing*, and I have frequently found it to be highly effective.

Besides the simple, open-hand style of banishing, there are many more involved types which employ incantations and ritual tools. These may help to develop a more immersive experience, which can facilitate a greater investment of intent and energy into the operation if it is needed. Ritual weapons are ideally suited for this purpose. Different traditions and schools of magic each have their own interpretation of this technique. Study them and find one that suits your needs, or even better, create your own using symbols that appeal to you. A simple example of this type of operation follows in Appendix A.

Manipulation

This operation is the one most characteristic of what quantum sorcery is about, the direct exertion of influence over probability in order to create the desired physical results. The idea is to create a superposition, then to resolve this state into the desired outcome via the process of decoherence. Depending on the favoured interpretation of quantum mechanical theory, this results in following the collapsing state vector into the universe where the desired result is manifest, or having the ensuing cascade of events propagating up from the microscale to the macroscale in the current phenomenal universe.

One way of visualising the instantiation of physical reality along the arrow of time is to picture a billiard ball rolling on a given course. You wish to alter the trajectory of this ball, but you only have a BB gun to use to do so. The best way to maximize the amount of change you can inflict on this ball is to hit it as early in its pathway as possible.

The removal of as many inhibiting factors as possible is vital to performing any form of magic. When not interfered with, reality follows the path of least resistance, and by using magic to alter this, the sorcerer is already placing a strain on the normal patterns of the universe. The tendency toward following the easiest path is true down to the level of fundamental particles themselves:

In quantum processes, a probability that something will happen is associated with the amount of energy required to make it happen. If an electron can move to one energy shell within the atom with very little expenditure of energy, and to another at very great expenditure of energy, the probability is very high that it will make the low-energy transition (Zohar, 1990).

As with others in this system of magic, the basis of this operation is the visualisation of the desired outcome. Whenever possible, this outcome should be constructed as one result of a binary choice in as much detail as is feasible under the conditions of the operation. If desired, this can be accompanied by any number of supportive techniques, such as the future/past writing, sigilization, or multimedia examples described in chapter two. This creates a conscious model of the outcome, which can then be distilled into a subconscious packet for transmission outward.

Lesser, more immediate examples of this skill which require only brief visualisations, include the influence of a random event such as a coin toss or a dice roll. This is often equated with psychokinesis, and the ambient resistance to the use of this ability in some circumstances is often high, particularly if others are unknowingly projecting their own subconscious desires to achieve their own desired result.

More involved manipulations may involve longer and more detailed visualisations and a build-up of personal energy until a desired threshold is reached, at which point the intent is projected. The actual moment of transmission should be like firing the intent outward like a projectile. It must be done with as much focus and intensity as possible. This is why altered states such as hypoxia, trance, and orgasm are used by many sorcerers. The effect of these states is to eliminate all rational thought for a brief moment in order to bypass the psychic censor, assuming that it has not been trained not to interfere through metaprogramming or other means.

Some magical systems emphasize that actions like this should be consciously forgotten after being performed. In my own exercises, I have found that practice is effective, but not completely essential. While it is detrimental to obsess on an outcome, long-term operations can actually be helped along by occasional bursts of supportive thought and energy, as long as such efforts are closely aligned with the original intent, and do not dilute it. Ultimately an operation either works, or it does not. If not, an analysis of factors which may have contributed to the lack of success can lead to better results in the future if properly acted upon.

Creating Virtual Constructs

This type of operation is used to create and maintain non-physical entities, objects, and locations for various purposes. Included in this broad category are the synthetic entities traditionally known as servitors, as well as structures which can be used to intensify the effects of visualisation. An example of how to create such an entity can be found in Appendix B.

Magical agents created to accomplish one or more specific tasks are known by several names, including thought forms, servitors, and *tulpas*. The basic process for the creation of these entities is that the specific task for which the being is being created is formulated, then that task is rendered into a symbol. One of the methods by which this encoding is done is through Spare's sigilisation technique described in chapter two. This symbol, along with another physical representation such as a small figurine, becomes the focus through which energy is invested into the entity. The purposes for which these entities are created are numerous, and may include tasks such as finding lost objects, serving as guardians, or committing acts of aggression.

The creation of an entity can be visualised as detaching a portion of the personal energy field and imbuing it with the desired task while focusing on the physical representations of its purpose and form. When the entity's purpose is fulfilled, or if it must be unmade prior to this for any reason, destroy the symbol(s) by which it was created, and re-absorb the energy which was invested in it.

Virtual structures are symbols through which magical potential may be stored, amplified, or directed. An example would be a purely visualised weapon or tool which has no material counterpart. Such items are useful as metaphors for various actions performed while visualising.

Summary

Employing the principles of quantum mechanics, wave physics, and chaos theory synthesized together through the use of metaphor and visualisation can help create an effective personal system of sorcery. With magic, try not to label any given approach as right or wrong, as the ultimate measure of the effectiveness of any magical system is whether or not it produces the results desired by its users.

Visualisation in this context refers to the creation of an internal mental model, whether purely visual or including other sensory simulation, to represent a real or virtual object or event. The development of this skill is essential to the practice of quantum sorcery, as it is through this faculty that microscopic models are created in order to be propagated outward to cause corresponding macroscopic states to be physically created in their images.

You can improve visualisation using several exercises. These include creating mental models of familiar objects and of an idealized self which can be used as an avatar in other visualisations which incorporate the self. The latter can also function as a model of self-improvement.

Develop an awareness of your personal energy field after becoming proficient in visualisation. This field is hybrid in nature, consisting of both the physical bioenergy field, and a virtual component which represents the capability to project the Will for magical operations. This portion of the field is largely a function of the mental state and the ability to circumvent the psychic censor. The intensity of the personal energy field can be increased or decreased through exercises which take in or bleed off virtual energy from the surrounding environment.

One can perform many basic magical operations by projecting the Will through visualisation of the personal energy field. These include the manipulation of probability and of personal and external energies for various purposes such as creating thought forms. Many of these operations can be done either with or without the addition of spoken incantations and ritual tools.

These examples and exercises are great starting points, but any operation which is constructed by the person using it, built on their own concepts of visualisation, and using their own symbol sets and tools is likely to be more effective than one created by someone else. Sorcery is ultimately the process by which an individual creates a magical link between the internal reality of the self and the external reality of the universe, and the creation of a personal set of tools and methods to establish and utilize this link is a fundamental step in this act.

Conclusion

In the intervening fifteen years since I first wrote the essay that became *Quantum Sorcery*, there have been numerous advances in the science that underpins this system. New discoveries in cosmology, particle physics, neuroscience, and other disciplines have accelerated, driven in part by stronger telescopes, more powerful computers, higher energy particle colliders, and more precise magnetic imaging.

Even as mankind has continued to acquire a greater understanding of the Universe around us, the usefulness of magic as a tool to contribute to this process has not diminished. In fact, as social and political unrest grip the globe, accompanied by climatic disruption and novel pathogens, the allure of old pathways is growing stronger, even as the prevalence of dogmatic, organized religion wanes. As in all times and places, we seek to find some framework or mechanism that will grant us some degree of control over our circumstances. Some seek power over others, some seek only to prevent themselves from being controlled.

To actualize one's own potential, one may need to employ a variety of tools and techniques. As new mental, emotional, and magical methods are learned, it is only natural to discard the old in favour of the new, or at least synthesize a completely different system from the disparate inputs. Like the Universe itself, mankind thrives on novelty. New experiences create new connections, on both the micro- and macro-cosmic scales. It is my hope that the techniques that I have described, and the glimpse of the underlying mechanism behind them will encourage further exploration and a hunger to dive deeper into the mysteries of existence.

Understand that magic works with probabilities and possibilities. The gap between impossible and improbable is vast. Learn to know the difference. Anticipate the possible outcomes and give reality a nudge toward the one most favourable to you. Walk in the world with open eyes. Be the sorcerer that you wish to be.

Appendix A
Claiming a Space

This is a simple banishing operation that is performed in order to create a space which resonates with the Will of its creator. This can be considered to be a pocket universe. In effect it is a virtual scalar field in which the state at all points in the space is dictated by the intent of the creator. This could be useful for banishing unwanted entities or energies prior to performing other operations, or as a defensive action in its own right. This was inspired by Peter Carroll's banishing ritual framework in *Liber Null*.

Although I use the term dagger throughout, any item which is used to focus and project is appropriate. I also assume that you hold the dagger in the right hand. If the left hand is used, then modify the directions accordingly. Begin by standing with feet shoulder width apart in the centre of the physical space which is to be claimed. Hold the dagger point-down next to the right thigh. Take several deep, relaxing breaths and bring the arm up to point at a 45-degree angle to the ground, held straight out from the right shoulder. The dagger should be held so that its length is in line with the arm. Speak in a clear, firm voice:

"By my Will I cleave the dimensions."

Sweep the dagger in a downward arc, ending the stroke pointing straight down beside the right leg. Visualise it cutting a rift in space-time and leaving a glowing trail in its wake. The colour of the visualised trail is subject to individual tastes, but I tend to see it as silver-white. Bring the dagger back up, pointing directly outward, arm parallel to the ground and perpendicular to the chest.

"I claim this space from the void."

Turn a full circle slowly clockwise in place, arm outstretched, sweeping the dagger parallel to the ground. As this is done, visualise another glowing beam projecting outward from its tip describing whatever distance and shape is desired. This beam leaves a trail in its wake, ending at the same place as this move was begun from, and intersecting the original rift. Return the feet to shoulder width and point the dagger straight up.

"As above..."

Sweep the arm down in an arc in until the tip of the dagger points downward toward the point of an equilateral triangle formed with the feet.

"...so below"

As the tip of the dagger sweeps, visualise the glowing trail previously created expanding as a shell into three dimensions, completely encompassing the claimed space in a nearly transparent but slightly luminous membrane.

"Within this space, I am the alpha and the omega."

Bring the right hand in so that the dagger is held in front of the face, perpendicular to the ground, and pointing up as in the salute given by fencers before beginning a bout.

"By my Will, it is done."

Return the dagger to its sheath or place it upon your altar.

To release the claimed space, resume the starting stance with feet at shoulder width and the dagger held point down next to the right thigh. Point the arm up at a 45-

degree angle, but this time, in front of the left shoulder rather than the right. Sweep it down diagonally from left to right until it is pointing down next to the right thigh.

"I release this space from my dominion."

Visualise the three-dimensional membrane fading out of existence. Take several deep breaths. Your working is complete.

Appendix B
Servitor Swarm Synergy

Following is an example of how to design and build a distributed virtual construct.

Of late I have been studying the phenomenon of distributed processing of function over networks, and the emergence of a superorganism which can result from the collective efforts of numerous components which are themselves quite simplistic. In biological systems, such as ant colonies, a hive mind emerges which coordinates the efforts of all its parts in a non-hierarchical yet efficient way. It is this effect which has inspired engineers to create swarming machines.

I began to contemplate whether or not a similar effect would occur if an interconnected swarm of servitors were created which were not individually invested with a great deal of intent, and were collectively charged with a broad statement of purpose

The result was that I decided to create a cluster of 12 identical servitors, which I refer to as *nodes*, each charged with the task of gathering information that would be of interest or benefit to me, and funnelling such information back to me by any convenient or available communication channel.

Collectively, the construct is designated as "Nexus 0xC", roughly meaning "the connected 12." I chose Hexadecimal, or base 16 to represent the numeric portion of the name in order to avoid the commonality of the everyday decimal numbering system. The individual component servitors are identically created from the same visualised seed which divides instantaneously into 12 equal parts. Upon the creation of the 12, each is intended to be self-aware, but is not yet connected to the others.

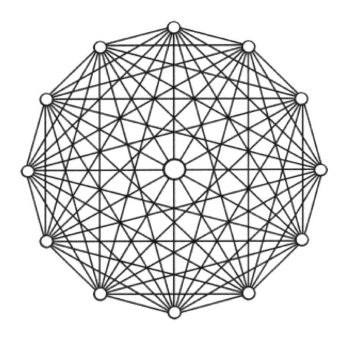

The symbol of the ultimate manifestation of Nexus 0xC is a dodecagon with an empty circle at each vertex. Each vertex is connected to every other in order to symbolize the network which exists between these servitors. In the centre of the network is another empty circle which represents me. Twelve identical tokens were also created to represent the nodes of the nexus, and to be the foci for the individual servitors. By design, these tokens are indistinguishable from one another, to emphasize the uniformity of the members of the swarm.

These tokens were deployed in various locations around the city to symbolize the wide scope of this information gathering system. As this was done, the servitors were visualised to emerge from the tokens as coherent, invisible wave forms, and to begin gathering information. This was to be stored until all nodes had been distributed and connected.

The physical components of this operation are accompanied by a corresponding set of visualised counterparts. The virtual seed form of the cluster was visualised as liquid silver-white light coalescing from the Void, accumulating into a mirrored, mercury-like sphere. Just as a larger glob of mercury accumulates smaller amounts into itself, increasing the volume of the sphere, the seed was allowed to develop in imaginal space. As each of the node servitors was released from its token, a portion of this energy was visualised to detach and emerge as the wave form of the servitor.

After the final token was distributed, the act of connecting them into the nexus was performed. The original dodecagon symbol was used as the focus for this operation. While focusing on the symbol, a state of excitatory gnosis was entered via a combination of sensory overload, mind-altering substances, and orgasm. At the moment immediately prior to white-out, I visualised a projection as emerging from the symbol as silver-white

Dave Smith

light and spreading out to connect the individual nodes. At this moment, all the nodes became joined through the myriad pathways into Nexus 0xC.

When I meditate and focus my thought on the Nexus symbol, I visualise myself as being within the centre hub of the network. If the swarm of node servitors has any information to relay to me, they can then do so through the pathways. I have only recently completed this operation, so I cannot yet report any demonstrable results.

The possibility of a hyper-implementation of this network might be a future extension of this construct, either as a group working, or in further iterations on my own. Additional clusters could be created, and then linked to the original to attain an even wider sensory array.

This material originally appeared in *Konton* Magazine, Vernal Equinox 2006, issue 3.1.

Glossary

Aion: (Greek) A long period of time, corresponding to a long lifespan.

Aiw: (Proto Indo-European) Vital force.

Alpha waves: Brain waves which range in frequency from 8.5 to 12 Hertz.

Alphabet of desire: A set of symbols created through automatic writing and meditation that have personal meaning for use in magical workings.

Alternity: An altered state of consciousness in which awareness of all possible courses in space-time is achieved.

Antiparticles: Companion particles proposed by Paul Dirac which have the same mass, but opposite charge, spin, and nuclear force of the fundamental particles.

Arrow of time: Symbolic representation of time as a uni-directional phenomenon due to the infinite entropy barrier which prevents time travel to the past.

Atom: First indivisible unit of matter proposed by Greek philosopher Democritus.

Attractor: A representative trajectory representing the stable state into which dynamic systems tend to settle into at some point in their development.

Bifurcation: A random divergence of trajectory in dynamic systems that are far from equilibrium.

Biophotons: Quanta of electromagnetic energy emitted by living cells.

Blackbody: An object that perfectly absorbs and emits all energy which strikes it.

Bosons: Force carrying particles including gravitons, gluons, photons, and W and Z bosons.

Brane: A multi-dimensional structure of varying size and energy that exists in a larger spatial dimension.

Bulk Space: Five-dimensional space-time in which interactions between branes are believed to occur.

Cascade: An effect which occurs when a perturbation or feedback causes effects which propagate across scales, from smaller systems up into larger systems.

Condensed phase: A phase of matter which occurs when a gas is cooled to near absolute zero. Particles in the resulting condensate share the same quantum state.

Consensus reality: The shared and generally agreed upon world in which humans interact with one another on the conscious level. It is constructed and maintained through the cumulative force of the world views of the participants.

Copenhagen Interpretation: Model of quantum theory proposed by Werner Heisenberg, Neils Bohr, and others in 1927.

Cosmic inflation: A theory proposed by Alan Guth which states that the early universe went through a stage of exponential expansion as it cooled.

Cosmology: The study of the structure and development of the universe.

Decoherence: The process by which a quantum system in

a state of superposition is collapsed into a single state to the exclusion of all other possible states.

Deterministic universe model: Model proposed by the Marquis de Laplace which states that if the state of the universe can be determined at any point in time, then a set of laws should exist which will allow the calculation of any prior or future state.

Electron: The fundamental particle of electromagnetic force.

Ekpyrotic universe: From the Greek ekpyrosis: A cosmological model in which the universe is cyclically consumed by, and reconstituted from, fire.

Engram: A theorized unit of discrete memory storage.

Entanglement: Phenomenon in which the quantum state of one particle is inextricably tied to the state of another subsequent to their interaction.

Entrainment: The imposition of a vibrational frequency onto one system by another.

Entropy: Thermodynamic principle that in any process in which energy is transferred, particularly as heat, some degree of the energy involved in the transfer will always be lost.

Eternal inflation: The process proposed by Andre Linde by which quantum fluctuations lead to a continuing exponential inflation of volumes in space which constitute new universes.

Evoke: To cause an entity to be manifest externally to the summoner.

Fermions: Matter particles such as the electron which have a spin of one-half.

Fourier transformation: (see spread function).

Fractal: From the Latin *fractus*: broken. A form of geometry expressed as a function in which features viewed at any level of magnification appear similar.

Fundamental forces: Four forces which describe the way in which matter interacts: gravitation, electromagnetism, the strong nuclear force, and the weak nuclear force.

Glossolalia: The vocalization of nonsensical sounds and phrases.

GUT: The grand unified theory, which would relate all four fundamental forces into a single model.

Harmonic: A frequency which is an integer multiple, such as two, three, etc. of the resonant frequency of a system.

Heisenberg's Uncertainty Principle: Principle that the precise position and momentum of a subatomic particle cannot both be known, as measuring one has an effect upon the other.

Hilbert Space: The theoretical space in which the functions which completely describe the states of quantum systems are manifest. Different Hilbert spaces can overlap spatially without interacting with one another.

Holomovement: The carrier wave by which the implicate order is transmitted.

Holonomic brain: Theory of consciousness proposed by Karl Pribram which states that the brain functions in a manner similar to a hologram, in that memory is stored not in discrete units, but is distributed throughout the whole structure.

Holy Guardian Angel: Alternately considered to be a literal guardian angel responsible for the protection and development of the magician, or as a personification of the higher self.

Hubble volume: The maximum visible extent of the phenomenal universe, approximately 4×10^{26} meters.

Implicate order: Cosmological theory of David Bohm which states that the true nature of existence is folded in on itself, and cannot be perceived until it unfolds, or explicates, into the phenomenal universe.

Iterative function: A function into which the results from previous calculations of the functions are fed to generate the next result.

Kia: The transcendental primal force proposed by Austin Osman Spare.

Laminar flow: A state of fluid flow characterized by regularity and a lack of turbulence.

Left Hand Path: Magical practices which seek to increase personal power through the usage of forces frequently labelled "evil" and considered to be in opposition to the God of Abraham.

Invoke: To cause an entity to be manifest internally to the summoner.

Leptons: A group of particles which take part in interactions of the weak nuclear force, such as protons,

Dave Smith

neurons, and electrons.

Lyapunov exponent: A function which calculates the ratio of two different solutions to a function and generates a number which indicates whether or not the trajectories generated from that function will diverge. A non-zero value indicates divergence between the trajectories.

M-theory: Theory proposed by Edward Witten which assumes the existence of 11 dimensions, ten of space and one of time, and incorporates strings and multi-dimensional branes as foundational structures of existence.

Macrocosm: (Greek) - *macros* (large) + *kosmos* (world).

Magical link: In sympathetic magic, a symbolic link between an object and its simulacrum through which effects on the object itself can be manifest by working them upon the simulacrum.

Meme: A replicator of cultural imitation and information.

Metaprogramming: The use of psychotropic substances and altered states of consciousness to enable mental self-reprogramming.

Microcosm: (Greek) - *micros* (small) + *kosmos* (world).

Microtubules: Tubular structures analogous to scaffolding which occur in the cytoskeleton of cells.

Mitogenic rays: Original name given to biophotons by Alexander Gurvich.

Multiverse: The collection of all possible parallel universes.

Neuroplasticity: The capability of neurons to form new connections or take on new functional roles.

Nodes: Points on a waveform which appear to stand still.

Nucleus: Centre structure of an atom composed of protons and neutrons, around which electrons orbit.

Operation: Generic term for a work of magic or sorcery.

Orgone: Life energy in the system theorized by psychoanalyst Wilhelm Reich.

Overself: The greater collective hyperconscious self proposed by Terence McKenna.

Phase space: A multi-dimensional graphing technique which displays the changes of graphed values over time.

Phenomenal reality: The four-dimensional (three of space, and one of time) world which is perceivable as the universal framework in which mankind exists.

Photon: A discrete, massless unit of energy, the quantum of electromagnetic force.

Planck length: 10^{-35} meters, the distance below which the smooth space-time model of general relativity breaks down into turbulence.

Planck's constant: The constant of proportionality between the frequency of a wave and its minimum energy, 1.05×10^{-27} gram-cm per second.

Pneuma: (Greek) The combination of the elements of air and fire.

Positron: The antiparticle of the electron.

Prana: Proto-matter from which energy is created.

Psychic censor: A mechanism of the conscious mind which determines, based on rules which have been internalized from consensus reality, what limits are placed on possibility.

Psychokinesis: The theorized human ability to manipulate matter and motion through the power of the mind.

Pumped system: A system into which energy is fed, or pumped, from an external source.

Quanta: Discrete packets of energy which constitute the smallest unit through which atoms can absorb or emit energy.

Quantum foam: Theorized state of turbulent matter and gravity which exists at scales smaller than 10^{-35} meters.

Quarks: Fundamental particles from which protons and neutrons are constructed.

Qi: (Mandarin) Breath.

Qi gong: (Mandarin) Breath work.

Relative state interpretation: Theory proposed by Hugh Everett, which states that any measurement of a quantum system will create a complex system in which the state of the system being measured can only be defined relative to the one measuring it.

Resonance: The state of two or more systems vibrating at the same frequency or at harmonic frequencies of one other.

Right Hand Path: Magical practices which seek to unite the magician with the Holy Guardian Angel. Stereotypically considered to be "good" magic.

Sacred alphabet: see *alphabet of desire*.

Scalar fields: dimensional areas to which a single numeric value for a measurable property is applied uniformly throughout their space.

Self metaprogrammers: Sentient conscious selves which arise from the complex of programs active within a human brain.

Sensitivity to initial conditions: Condition of nonlinear systems whose behaviour patterns diverge at some point due to slight alterations to their starting values.

Servitor: see *thought form*.

Sigils: Statements of desire which have been rendered into symbols via the combination of words into graphical forms for transmission to the subconscious mind and then out into the universe where their intent can be manifest.

Similarity and contagion: The beliefs that like attracts or effects like, and that an item which is a part of, or has been in contact with, another object takes on some of that other object's properties.

Sorcery: The manipulation of probability and energy through the use of symbols and directed Will to alter phenomenal reality to bring about changes or circumstances desired by the sorcerer.

Sortilege: The practice of divining the future by reading lots.

Spin: Property of fundamental particles which is analogous to angular velocity, or the rate at which the particle is envisioned to spin around an axis.

Spread function: A mathematical function spatial coordinates can be converted into frequencies.

Standard Model of particle physics: Collective theory encompassing all fundamental particles and the non-gravitational forces.

State vector: The mathematical expression of the waveform of a quantum which collapses upon observation.

Strange attractor: A point in the phase space of chaotic systems toward which trajectories graphed are similar, but never identically repeat.

Stochastic: Denotes systems which contain a random variable which makes predicting the behaviour of the system over time difficult or impossible.

String theory: Theory which represents the smallest components of matter as 1-dimensional vibrating filaments rather than as point particles.

Subliminal seed space: Robert Jahn's term for the deepest level of existence at which the division between mental and physical phenomena breaks down into a continuum of information.

Superposition: State of a quantum system which has not yet had its state vector collapsed. All outcomes are possible.

Sympathetic magic: Magic based on the principles of similarity and contagion, that a portion or simulacrum of a thing allows a magical link or conduit to be created through which that thing can be affected by manipulating the simulacrum.

System: A group of interrelated elements related by function which forms a complex whole.

Thought form: A pseudo-autonomous psychic entity, either pre-existing or willed into existence. This entity may be created for a specific task, or for more general purposes.

Tulpa: An entity or object created by Will and thought in Tibetan mythology.

Upanishad: (Sanskrit) One of a collection of philosophical writings which comment on the earlier Vedas of the Hindu religion.

Vitalism: Philosophy which contains the belief that mechanical processes are inadequate to explain life and that a vital energy must also be present to explain it.

Works Cited

Abe, K., Akutsu, R., Ali, A. et al. "Constraint on the matter–antimatter symmetry-violating phase in neutrino oscillations." *Nature*: 580, 339–344 , April 15, 2020.

Aspect, Alain. "Bell's Inequality Test: More Ideal Than Ever." *Nature*: 398, March 18, 1999.

Bardon, Franz. *Initiation Into Hermetics: A Course of Instruction of Magic Theory & Practice.* Trans A. Radspieler. Wuppertal, West Germany: Dieter Ruggeberg: 1971 ed.

Barrett, Jeffrey. "Everett's Relative-State Formulation of Quantum Mechanics." in Edward N. Zalta ed., *The Stanford Encyclopedia of Philosophy. Spring* 2003 edition.

Bey, Hakim. "T. A. Z. - The Temporary Autonomous Zone." Brooklyn: Autonomedia: 1985.

Biraco, Joel. "How the Chaos Current Died." *KAOS*: 14, April 2002.

Blumetti, Robert. *Vril: The Life Force of the Gods.* New York: iUniverse: 2010.

Bohm, David. *Wholeness and the Implicate Order.* London and New York: Routledge: 1980.

Brown, David Jay and Novick, Rebecca McClen, "From Here to Alternity and Beyond." in *Mavericks of the Mind.* Internet edition (www.levity.com/mavericks): 1991.

Carroll, Peter. *Liber Null & Psychonaut.* York Beach: Weiser: 1987.

Carroll, Peter. *PsyberMagick.* Tempe: New Falcon: 1995.

Collier, John and Burch, Mark. "Symmetry, Levels and Entrainment." *Proceedings of the International Society for Systems Sciences*: 2000.

Coveney, Peter. "Chaos, entropy, and the arrow of time." in Nina Hall, ed., *Exploring Chaos*. London: Norton: 1991.

Crowley, Aleister. *Magic In Theory and Practice*. New York: Castle: 1929.

Dawkins, Richard. *The Selfish Gene*. Oxford: University of Oxford Press: 1976.

Defoe, Daniel. *A History of the Black Art*. London: J. Roberts: 1727.

Deutsch, David. "The Structure of the Multiverse." *Proceedings of the Royal Society* A458 2028 2911-23 (2002).

Deutsch, David and Hayden, Patrick. "Information Flow in Entangled Quantum Systems." *Proceedings of the Royal Society* A456, 1759-1774 (2000).

Edwards, Jonathan. "Is Consciousness Only a Property of Individual Cells?" *Journal of Consciousness Studies* April/May: 2005.

Fröhlich, Herbert. "This Week's Citation Classic: Long Range Coherence and Energy Storage in Biological Systems." *Current Contents* 19: May 9, 1988.

Gardner, Martin. "David Bohm and Jiddo Krishnamurti." *Skeptical Inquirer*, July, 2000,

Gifford, George. A Discourse of the Subtill Practises of Devilles by Witches and Sorcerers. London: Toby Cooke: 1587.

Dave Smith

Gleick, James. *Chaos*. New York: Penguin: 1987.

Greene, Brian. *The Elegant Universe*. New York: Norton: 1999.

Guth, Alan. "Was Cosmic Inflation the 'Bang' of the Big Bang?" *The Beamline*: 27. 1997.

Hall, Manly P. *The Secret Teachings of all Ages*. Los Angeles: Philosophical Research Society: 1928.

Hameroff, Stuart and Penrose, Roger. "Orchestrated Objective Reduction of Quantum Coherence in Brain Microtubules: The "Orch OR" Model for Consciousness", http://www.quantumconsciousness.org/penrose-hameroff/orchOR.html. 1996.

Hawking, Stephen. A Brief History of Time. New York: Bantam: 1988.

Hawkins, Jaq D. "Austin Osman Spare - The Nescient Father of Chaos." http://www.jaqdhawkins.com/fatherofchaos.php. 1996.

Heisenberg, Werner. "The Copenhagen Interpretation of Quantum Theory." in Timothy Ferris ed. *The World Treasury of Physics, Astronomy and Mathematics*. New York: Little, Brown & Co.: 1991.

Hole, John W. *Human Anatomy and Physiology*. Dubuque: Wm. C. Brown: 1984.

Holmstrom, Laurel. "Self-Identification with Deity and Voces Magicae in Ancient Egyptian and Greek Magic." http://www.hermetic.com/pgm/self-identify.html. 1998.

Huth, A., de Heer, W., Griffiths, T. et al. "Natural speech

reveals the semantic maps that tile human cerebral cortex." Nature 532, 453–458 (2016). https://doi.org/10.1038/nature17637.

Jahn, Robert and Dunne, Brenda. "A Modular Model of Mind/Matter Manifestations (M^5)." *Journal of Scientific Exploration*, 15:3. 2001.

Jahn, Robert and Dunne, Brenda. "Science of the Subjective." *Journal of Scientific Exploration*, 11:2. 1997.

Joines, William T. et al. "The Measurement and Characterization of Charge Accumulation and Electromagnetic Emission from Bioenergy Healers." *Parapsychological Association Convention Research Brief.* 2004.

Khoury, Justin et al. "The Ekpyrotic Universe: Colliding Branes and the Origin of the Hot Big Bang." *High Energy Physics*, 15 Aug 2001.

Kong, Jia et al. "Measurement-induced, spatially-extended entanglement in a hot, strongly-interacting atomic system." *Nature Communications*, 11, 2415 (2020).

Levi, Eliphas. *Dogme et Rituel de la Haute Magie*. England: Rider & Company, 1896.

Lilly, John C. *Programming and Metaprogramming in the Human Biocomputer* 2nd ed. New York: Three Rivers Press. 1972.

Linde, Andrei. "The Self-Reproducing Inflationary Universe." *Scientific American*. November 1994.

Lorenz, Edward N. "Deterministic Nonperiodic Flow." *Journal of the Atmospheric Sciences*: 20: March 1963, 130-41.

Maltz, Maxwell. *Psycho-Cybernetics Deluxe Edition*. New

Dave Smith

York: TarcherPerigee. 2016.

Mandelbrot, Benoit. "How Long is the Coast of Britain?" *Science*: 156, 1967.

May, Robert. "The Chaotic Rhythms of Life." in Nina Hall, ed., *Exploring Chaos*. London: Norton: 1991.

McKenna, Terence. "New Maps of Hyperspace." *Freakbeat* 7 45-47;54. 1990.

Mishlove, Jeffrey. "The Holographic Brain." interview with Karl Pribram. http://www.intuition.org/txt/pribram.htm. 1998.

Mutnick, Peter. "Hot Discussion with Jack Sarfatti on Bohm Theory." http://www.geocities.com/saint7peter/HotDiscussionw ithSarfatti.html.

Nelson, Roger D. "The Physical Basis of Intentional Healing Systems." *PEAR Technical Report 99001*. January 1999.

Niemark, Jill. "Good and Evil at the Planck Scale" interview with Stuart Hameroff. *Nexus.* http://www.metanexus.net/metanexus_online/show_ar ticle.asp?7736. 2003.

O'Connor, J. J. and Robertson, E. F. "A History of Quantum Mechanics." www-groups.dcs.st-and.ac.uk/~history/ HistTopics/The_Quantum_age_begins.html. 1996.

Princeton Engineering Anomalies Research homepage. http://www.princeton.edu/~pear/.

Pesce, Mark. "Church of the Motherfucker." in Russ Kick

ed. *You are Being Lied To*. New York: The Disinformation Company Ltd. 2000.

Pietsch, Paul. "Hologramic Mind." *Quest* 77.

Planck, Max. "The Second Law of Thermodynamics." in Timothy Ferris ed. *The World Treasury of Physics, Astronomy and Mathematics*. New York: Little, Brown & Co. 1991.

Popp, Fritz-Albert. "About the Coherence of Biophotons." *Macroscopic Quantum Coherence Conference Proceedings*. 1999.

Popp, Fritz-Albert. "Biophysical Aspects of the Psychic Situation." *International Institute of Biophysics*. 2006.

Pratt, David. "David Bohm and the Implicate Order." *Sunrise*. February/March 1993.

Prigogene, Ilya and Stengers, Isabelle. *Order out of Chaos*. New York: Bantam: 1984.

Rubik, Beverly and Jabs, Harry, "Effects of Intention, Energy Healing, and Mind-Body States on Biophoton Emission" *Cosmos and History: The Journal of Natural and Social Philosophy* Vol. 13, no. 2, 2017.

Schroeder, Manfred. *Fractals, Chaos, Power Laws.* New York: W.H. Freeman: 1991.

Schwartz, Jeffrey M. and Begley, Sharon. *The Mind & The Brain: Neuroplasticity and the Power of Mental Force*. New York: Harper Perennial: 2002.

Seligmann, Kurt. *The Mirror of Magic*: A History of Magic in the Western World. New York: Pantheon: 1948.

Shah , Idres. *The Sufis.* New York: Anchor: 1971.

Shannon, C. E., "A Mathematical Theory of Communication." *Bell System Technical Journal.* Vol. 27, pp. 379–423, 623–656, July/October, 1948.

Sherwin, Ray. *Vitriol.* East Morton, Yorkshire, UK: Morton Press: 2015.

Spare, Austin Osman. *The Book of Pleasure (Self-Love) The psychology of Ecstacy.* (1913). Montreal: 93 Publishing: 1975 ed.

Spare, Austin Osman and Carter, Frederick. "Automatic Drawing." *Form*: 1, 1916.

Stenger, Victor J. "Mystical Physics: Has Science Found the Path to the Ultimate?" *Free Inquiry.* 16(3)1996.

Tegmark, Max. "Parallel Universes." in John D. Barrow, Paul C.W. Davies and Charles L. Harper, Jr. eds. *Science and Ultimate Reality: From Quantum to Cosmos.* Cambridge: Cambridge University Press: 2004.

Tegmark, Max. "The Importance of Quantum Decoherence in Brain Processes." *Physical Review E,* 50: Nov 1999.

Thorsson, Edred. *A Book of Troth.* St. Paul, MN: Llewellyn Publications: 1989.

Tiller, W.A., Dibble, W.E. Jr, Nunley R., Shealy, C.N. "Toward general experimentation and discovery in conditioned laboratory spaces: Part I. Experimental pH change findings at some remote sites." *Journal of alternative and complementary medicine.* 10(1):145-57 Feb 2004.

Turing, A.M. "Computing Machinery and Intelligence."

Mind: October 1950 436-42.

Tyson, Donald. *Three Books of Occult Philosophy*. St. Paul, MN: Llewellyn Publications: 1992.

von Neumann, John. *The Computer and the Brain*. New Haven: Yale University Press: 1958.

Weihs, G., et al. "Violation of Bell's inequality under strict Einstein locality conditions." *Physical Review Letters*, 81: 1998.

Wolfram, Stephan. *A New Kind of Science*. Champaign, Il: Wolfram Media: 2002.

Woolf, Nancy J. and Hameroff, Stuart R. "A Quantum Approach to Visual

Consciousness." *Trends in Cognative Sciences*. Vol 5 No. 11, November 2001.

Zohar,Danah. *The Quantum Self*. New York: Quill: 1990.

About the Author

Frequently known as Vargr23 among online and magical communities, Dave Smith has been studying and practicing magic in various forms for over 30 years. He was the founder of the Grove of Oakhaven, the Lawspeaker of the Northstar Kindred, and a founding elder of the Indiana Asatru Council. His articles and reviews have appeared in the journals *Konton* and *Idunna*, as well as on his website SpikeVision (www.spikevision.org).

He has indulged his lifelong love of information by working in a science library, an astronomical observatory, and as a data architect. Along the way, he has also been a brewer, leatherworker, performance artist, and sideshow crewman.

He graduated from Indiana State University in 1993, and currently lives in Indianapolis, Indiana.

Other Titles by Dave Smith:

Voidworking: Practical Sorcery from Primordial Nothingness, Megalithica Books, UK, 2020.

Recent Titles from Megalithica Books

Coming Forth by Day by Storm Constantine

This book explores the myths of Ancient Egyptian gods and goddesses – showing how their stories relate to aspects of our lives, hopes and aspirations, and how we can learn from these ancient narratives. Through 28 deep and evocative pathworkings and rituals, the author provides a rich and vivid system of magic that the practitioner – whether experienced or a novice – can utilize in the search for self-knowledge, and to help themselves, others and the world around them. ISBN: 978-1-912241-11-8 Price: £12.99, $16.99

SHE: Primal Meetings with the Dark Goddess by Storm Constantine & Andrew Collins

The Dark Goddess is unpredictable, dispassionate, cruel, and often deadly. She reflects our deepest desires, fears, hopes and expectations. In this fully-illustrated book, Storm Constantine and Andrew Collins have selected a fascinating range of 34 goddesses, including some who are not so well-known. The pathworkings to meet them and explore their realms will offer insight into these often-misunderstood deities. (This title is also available as a limited edition, numbered hardback.) ISBN: 978-1-912241-06-4 Price: £12.99, $18.99

Voidworking by Dave Smith

Voidworking is a system of practical sorcery that draws upon the primordial state of being as a source of power and inspiration for performing acts of Will. This work examines various conceptions of the Void, from ancient religion to modern pop culture to gain a better understanding of how this realm of limitless potential can be embraced rather than feared. Magical techniques, including binding, banishing, evocation, scrying, and others are described that tap into a largely overlooked wellspring of energy that has long been thought to be the purview of divinity. ISBN: 978-1-912241-17-0 Price: £9.99, $13.99

Dave Smith

Recent Titles from Immanion Press

A Wolf at the Door by Tanith Lee

 Includes 13 tales, most of which appeared only in magazines or rare anthologies. "A wolf at the door" implies hidden threat – until the door is open, we don't really know what's out there. And now the beast is upon you, scratching at the wood, its hot breath steaming on the step. Will you survive the encounter? Perhaps, once the door is opened, what you might have thought to be a threat turns out to be something else entirely. But of course, it can also be a werewolf…

ISBN 978-1-912815-04-3, £11.99, $15.99 pbk

Breathe, My Shadow by Storm Constantine

 A standalone Wraeththu Mythos novel. Seladris believes he carries a curse making him a danger to any who know him. Now a new job brings him to Ferelithia, the town known as the Pearl of Almagabra. But Ferelithia conceals a dark past, which is leaking into the present. In the strange old house, Inglefey, Seladris tries to deal with hauntings of his own and his new environment, until fate leads him to the cottage on the shore where the shaman Meladriel works his magic. Has Seladris been drawn to Ferelithia to help Meladriel repel a malevolent present or is he simply part of the evil that now threatens the town?

ISBN: 978-1-912815-06-7 £13.99, $17.99 pbk

The Lord of the Looking Glass by Fiona McGavin

 The author has an extraordinary talent for taking genre tropes and turning them around into something completely new, playing deftly with topsy-turvy relationships between supernatural creatures and people of the real world. "Post Garden Centre Blues" reveals an unusual relationship between taker and taken in a twist of the changeling myth. "A Tale from the End of the World" takes the reader into her developing mythos of a post-apocalyptic world, which is bizarre, Gothic and steampunk all at once. Following in the tradition of exemplary short story writers like Tanith Lee and Liz Williams, Fiona has a vivid style of writing that brings intriguing new visions to fantasy, horror and science fiction. ISBN: 978-1-907737-99-2, £11.99, $17.50 pbk

Ingram Content Group UK Ltd.
Milton Keynes UK
UKHW010610130623
423358UK00004B/151